D1313862

ILLUSTRATED TRANSPORT ENCYCLOPEDIA

FIGHTER AIRCRAFT OF WORLD WARS I & II

ILLUSTRATED TRANSPORT ENCYCLOPEDIA

FIGHTER AIRCRAFT OF WORLD WARS I & II

Featuring photographs from the Imperial War Museum

FRANCIS CROSBY

LORENZ BOOKS

This book is dedicated to my wife Vanessa and daughter Gemma, for their help and understanding while I was engrossed in writing this, and to my parents who always encouraged me to learn.

This edition is published by Lorenz Books

Lorenz Books is an imprint of Anness Publishing Ltd
Hermes House, 88–89 Blackfriars Road, London SE1 8HA
tel. 020 7401 2077; fax 020 7633 9499
www.lorenzbooks.com; info@anness.com

UK agent: The Manning Partnership Ltd,
6 The Old Dairy, Melcombe Road, Bath BA2 3LR;
tel. 01225 478444; fax 01225 478440; sales@manning-partnership.co.uk

UK distributor: Grantham Book Services Ltd,
Isaac Newton Way, Alma Park Industrial Estate, Grantham, Lincs NG31 9SD;
tel. 01476 541080; fax 01476 541061; orders@gbs.tbs-ltd.co.uk

North American agent/distributor: National Book Network,
4501 Forbes Boulevard, Suite 200, Lanham, MD 20706;
tel. 301 459 3366; fax 301 429 5746; www.nbnbooks.com

Australian agent/distributor: Pan Macmillan Australia,
Level 18, St Martins Tower, 31 Market St, Sydney, NSW 2000;
tel. 1300 135 113; fax 1300 135 103; customer.service@macmillan.com.au

New Zealand agent/distributor: David Bateman Ltd,
30 Tarndale Grove, Off Bush Road, Albany, Auckland;
tel. (09) 415 7664; fax (09) 415 8892

A CIP catalogue record for this book is available from the British Library.

Publisher: Joanna Lorenz
Managing Editor: Judith Simons
Project Editor: Felicity Forster
Designer: Steve West
Copy Editors: Peter Moloney and
Alan Thatcher
Production Controller: Darren Price

Previously published as part of a larger volume, *Fighter Aircraft*

1 3 5 7 9 10 8 6 4 2

Contents

Introduction

"It is not to be expected that aircraft will be able to carry out their duties undisturbed. In war, advantages must be fought for and the importance of aerial reconnaissance is so great that each side will strive to prevent the other side making use of it." Royal Flying Corps manual, 1914.

This observation predates the first true fighter aircraft but neatly sums up how fighter aircraft came to be. World War I reconnaissance aircraft, "scouts", began to gather increasingly valuable information for their forces and effective armament became a necessity so they could carry out their work unmolested. Initially scout crews armed themselves to take the occasional shot at other scouts. The aeroplane, once no more than a sporting contraption, had become a weapon, and a special type of military aircraft soon evolved – the fighter.

From simple beginnings over the bloody trenches of World War I, fighter aircraft developed into the extraordinarily complex machines in service at the end of World War II. Although air fighting is only a phenomenon of the last century, it became central to securing military victory on the ground. In 1940, Hitler's Luftwaffe needed to gain control of the sky over southern England before Germany could mount an effective invasion of Britain. Without air superiority Germany risked their ground troops coming under constant attack from British bombers. The fighters of Britain's Royal Air Force defended their country's sky in what has become an almost legendary

TOP: The Hurricane (top) and Spitfire, two of World War II's classic fighting aircraft. ABOVE: A classic fighter pilot pose – an RAF pilot with his Curtiss P-40 Kittyhawk.

campaign in the summer of 1940 – The Battle of Britain – and Germany's planned invasion was thwarted.

The weapons with which the Spitfires and Messerschmitts fought each other during the Battle of Britain would have been recognized by the pilots from World War I – machine-guns and cannon, the latter basically a heavy machine-gun that fired explosive shells. Pilots from both wars would however have almost seen "the whites of their eyes" when in combat with an enemy, in contrast to the fire-and-forget air combat environment of today, dominated by "smart" weapons.

In terms of pilot workload, the newer fighters in service at the end of World War II were very demanding, and a world away from their World War I predecessors. Advances in aerodynamic research led to aircraft such as the Spitfire and the Messerschmitt 163 and 262, which not only looked very different to the Great War fighters but also travelled at much greater speeds. These shifts to monoplanes, enclosed cockpits and retractable undercarriages were fundamental advances that marked the difference between the two World Wars.

This book attempts to tell the story of fighter aircraft and how they evolved, and highlights particular episodes of history in which fighters have played a key role, such as the Battle of Britain in 1940. The A–Z listing of fighters does not claim to include every fighter of the time. Instead it presents the individual stories of what the author believes to be the most significant fighters. Specification tables are presented in a consistent manner to enable the reader to readily compare size, weights and capability of aircraft as diverse as the Fokker Dr.I, the P-51 Mustang and the Hawker Fury monoplane. The performance figures quoted in the table for each type should be seen as broad indicators of an aircraft's capabilities. Aircraft performance and capability can vary considerably, even within the same marks of an aircraft type. If drop tanks are fitted, for example, maximum speed can be reduced – even radio aerials can affect performance. Also, the maximum speeds quoted are top speeds achieved at the optimum altitude for that particular aircraft type and should not be seen as the definitive top speed for an aircraft at all altitudes.

Key to flags

For the specification boxes, the national flag that was current at the time of the aircraft's use is shown.

Australia

Britain

Czechoslovakia

France

Germany: World War I

Germany: World War II

Italy

Japan

Netherlands

Poland

Romania

USA

USSR

LEFT: **The Messerschmitt Bf109 was perhaps the definitive German fighter of World War II.**

The History of World War Fighter Aircraft

The fighter aircraft, born in World War I, played a crucial role in that conflict and in World War II. Fighter aircraft have won wars, prevented wars and defended nations from aggressors. Through continuous development, the high performance fighters in action at the end of World War II, such as the P-51 Mustang and Focke-Wulf 190, were a far cry from the scout aircraft that exchanged pistol shots over the trenches of World War I. Nevertheless, the success of these ultimate piston fighters still relied upon the pilot being a good shot, that most basic hunting skill.

Thanks to engine developments, the speed of fighter aircraft increased remarkably from World War I through to the mid-1940s, but agility and firepower were equally important to designers and the air forces they equipped.

The development of the fighter was vital. Fighters were used to protect a nation's airspace, escort bomber aircraft and, in the case of some early multi-role aircraft, carry out reconnaissance or ground attack missions. Air superiority became a military necessity and the fighter aircraft was able to provide this to military strategists.

LEFT: **The Fokker Dr.I Triplane, forever associated with the Red Baron, Manfred von Richthofen.**

Birth of the fighter

TOP: **The Wright Brothers, Wilbur (second from left) and Orville (far right) and their Wright Military Aeroplane, 1909.**

ABOVE: **Lt Harvey-Kelly's B.E.2a was the first British aircraft to land in France after World War I began.**

Although the Wright Brothers pioneered sustained and controllable powered flight in 1903, they were not the first builders of military aircraft. The first contract for a military aeroplane was awarded to Frenchman Clément Ader in February 1892 for the construction of a two-seater capable of lifting a 75kg/165lb bombload. The aircraft failed to fly but the precedent was set – the military were interested in the aeroplane as a weapon.

In 1907 the US Army released the first ever specification for a military aeroplane issued for commercial tender. Within the specification were the requirements that the aircraft should have a speed of at least 64kph/40mph and that it should be designed to carry two persons having a combined weight of 159kg/350lb for 201km/125 miles.

A key year in the development of military air power was 1910. Missiles were first dropped from an aeroplane in January 1910 when Lt Paul Beck of the US Army released sandbags representing bombs over the city of Los Angeles, but, more importantly for this book, the first military firearm to be fired from an aeroplane was a rifle used by Lt Jacob Earl Fickel of the United States Army from a two-seat Curtiss biplane on August 20, 1910. Equally significant was a German patent, taken out in 1910, for a device that allowed a fixed machine-gun to be fired from an aeroplane.

The first British aeroplane built as an armed fighting machine was the Vickers Destroyer E.F.B.1 ordered by the British Admiralty in November 1912. A year later, in November 1913, the first aerial combat between aircraft took place during the Mexican civil war – pistol shots were exchanged and, although none seemed to hit the mark, the aircraft was now seen as a weapon of war. But at the outbreak of World War I, military aircraft had a long way to go before they could be described as effective fighting machines.

When World War I broke out in 1914, Britain's Royal Flying Corps had five squadrons. Most of these B.E.2s, Blériot monoplanes, Farman biplanes, Avro 504s and B.E.8s were sent to France in mid-August 1914 – all were unarmed. Blériot had conquered the English Channel just five years earlier and crossing that expanse of water to France by air was still a risky undertaking. When the first Royal Naval Air Service aircraft arrived in France in late August they were promptly fired on by their own troops. British Union Jack flags were quickly painted beneath the wings of British aircraft, being soon replaced by the roundels developed for the Allies.

Arming these early military aircraft was not easy, and a stray friendly bullet could have easily damaged a vital bracing wire or wooden support, not to mention the wooden propeller. At first, aircrew were armed with hand-held weapons – pistols and rifles. Early use of machine-guns like the Lewis gun was not immediately successful as the weapon's weight severely hampered the aircraft's performance. On August 22, 1914 RFC aircraft were scrambled to challenge a German Albatros – a Farman armed with a Lewis Gun took half an hour to reach 305m/1000ft and on landing the pilot was ordered to remove the Lewis and carry only a rifle. Machine-guns were however soon acknowledged to be the best armament and were gradually fitted to the sturdier aircraft entering service on both sides of World War I.

Mounted cavalry did see action early in World War I but the mechanized battlefield was no place for these warriors of another age and the mounted cavalry were driven from the field of combat forever. By early 1915, aircraft began to take over the reconnaissance role of the cavalry. Whereas cavalry could not ride through enemy positions defended by barbed wire and machine-guns, aircraft could simply fly over these positions and gather intelligence about the enemy – the military aircraft was beginning to define its role.

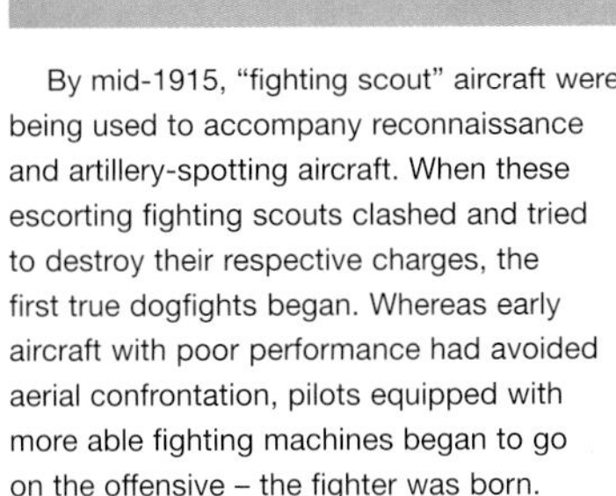

TOP: **This dramatic painting of World War I combat shows aircraft attacking out of the sun.** ABOVE: **The Sopwith Camel was another classic British fighter – note the guns, synchronized to fire between the spinning propeller blades.** LEFT: **The Bristol Fighter's arrival over the Western Front was bad news for enemy aircrews.** BELOW: **The Albatros D.Va was the ultimate Albatros D. fighter but was soon outclassed as better Allied aircraft appeared to counter it.**

By mid-1915, "fighting scout" aircraft were being used to accompany reconnaissance and artillery-spotting aircraft. When these escorting fighting scouts clashed and tried to destroy their respective charges, the first true dogfights began. Whereas early aircraft with poor performance had avoided aerial confrontation, pilots equipped with more able fighting machines began to go on the offensive – the fighter was born.

The first aces

World War I was a conflict fought on a truly massive scale – the devastation and loss of life on all sides was fantastically high. Almost as an antidote to the grim reports of mass slaughter, the stories of daring pilots in their magnificent machines, locked in aerial combat with a deadly foe, gripped the people back home on all sides of the conflict. The new knights were the men who did battle flying the new, dangerous yet glamorous aeroplane.

Albert Ball – Britain

Ball was the first British ace idolized by the public and was the darling of the British press. An engineering student when the war began, he transferred from the regular army to the Royal Flying Corps in 1915. From his arrival in France in February 1916, Ball established a reputation as a fearless pilot and excellent shot, achieving his first confirmed victory in late June. In just three months over the Somme, he scored 30 victories. With the introduction of the S.E.5, he reluctantly gave up his Nieuport XVII and on May 6, 1917 claimed his 44th and last victim, a German Albatros D.III.

The S.E.5s of Ball's flight encountered Manfred von Richthofen's unit, the all-red Jasta 11 on the evening of May 7, 1917 and Ball was last seen entering a thundercloud. Moments before Ball crashed, a German officer on the ground witnessed Ball's undamaged inverted aircraft emerge alone from the clouds, 61m/200ft above the ground with a dead propeller. He was only 20 years old and was posthumously awarded the Victoria Cross. Ball's death profoundly affected the morale of the Royal Flying Corps.

Manfred von Richthofen – Germany

The most famous ace of World War I, Manfred von Richthofen, joined a cavalry regiment in 1911. He transferred to the German Air Service in May 1915, initially as an observer, and earned his pilot's wings in December that year. After brief service on the Russian Front he transferred to France in August 1916 and on September 17, 1916 claimed the first of his 80 confirmed victories.

On January 16, 1917 he was given command of his own squadron, Jagdstaffel 11 and on June 26 that year, the command of Jagdgeschwader 1, a wing of four staffeln (squadrons) that came to be known as Richthofen's Flying Circus. The wing was made up of Germany's flying élite and Richthofen was keen to let the enemy know they were dealing with the "top guns" of the time – his personal Albatros D.III was painted all red and his men's aircraft were equally conspicuous, earning him the Red Baron nickname. Richthofen was almost killed in a dogfight in July 1917 – he received a serious head wound but managed to crash-land his Albatros D.V. On September 2, 1917, flying the new Fokker Dr.I triplane, he scored his 60th kill. The Red Baron's score continued to climb and on April 20, 1918 he claimed his 80th and last victim, an RAF Sopwith

TOP: **Captain Albert Ball VC, DSO, MC – Britain's first aviation hero of the Great War.** ABOVE: **The Albatros D.V was the type being flown by the "Red Baron" in mid-1917.** RIGHT: **Pilots of Jagdstaffel 11 with von Richthofen in the cockpit of the Albatros D.III.**

Camel. Richthofen was killed the next day as he flew over the trenches in pursuit of Canadian Wilfrid May in his R.E.8. Evidence suggests Richthofen was hit by a single bullet, possibly fired from a machine-gun in the trenches. Richthofen's loss devastated German morale and far outweighed the military value of any further victories he might have achieved.

Edward Rickenbacker – USA

A celebrated racing driver before World War I, Eddie Rickenbacker first went to France in 1917 as the personal chauffeur of General Pershing. Eager to see action, he transferred to the US Army Aviation Section, initially as an engineering officer. After learning to fly, he joined the 94th Aero Squadron in March 1918.

He first flew Nieuport 28s and then SPADs and by the end of the war he had built up the impressive total of 26 victories, even more remarkable as he was hospitalized for two of his eight months of combat flying. Rickenbacker took over as commanding officer of the 94th in September 1918, and having been born in 1890, Rickenbacker was an old man compared to many of the pilots he commanded. Unlike many other famous World War I fighter pilots, he survived the war and returned to a hero's welcome in the USA as America's leading fighter ace.

Charles Nungesser – France

Like Rickenbacker, Charles Nungesser had been a racing driver, and by the end of World War I Nungesser was officially France's third-ranking fighter ace. While racing in South America, the Frenchman learned to fly and on returning to France in 1914 he joined the army. Nungesser got a transfer to the Flying Service and by 1915 he was a reconnaissance pilot, albeit a very aggressive example. In November that year he was posted to a fighter squadron and began to build his impressive total of 45 victories, most of which he won flying Nieuports bearing his favoured skull and crossbones motif.

On January 29, 1916 Nungesser was in a serious crash and broke both legs, but he was flying again within two months. He was wounded many times and in-between his numerous crashes and visits to the hospital, Nungesser was taking his toll of German aircraft – by December 1916, a total of 21 victories.

At one point a German aircraft dropped a message on his aerodrome challenging him to a "duel". When Nungesser arrived at the appointed place he was ambushed by six German fighters. He shot two of them down and the others fled. On the same day, the Frenchman was attacked in the air by an RFC pilot who clearly had poor recognition skills – the British pilot persisted and Nungesser reluctantly shot him down too. The sky over the Western Front was full of danger. By mid-August 1917 he was so physically exhausted that he had to be carried to his aircraft, such was his desire to fight. Nungesser continued the familiar pattern of crashes, injuries and more victories until the war's end.

Although he survived the war, he disappeared over the Atlantic in 1927 while trying to fly from France to the USA.

TOP: The Fokker Dr.I Triplane was von Richthofen's last mount. ABOVE: With his matinee idol looks and outstanding combat record, Eddie Rickenbacker was the all-American hero. LEFT: Pictured with his Nieuport, Nungesser started the war as a cavalry officer and began his military flying in 1915.

LEFT: **The cockpit of this Bristol Scout replica is equipped with all the original instruments a 1914 pilot had.** BELOW: **Woodworking tools outnumbered metalworking tools in the early aircraft factories.** BOTTOM: **With two wings generating more lift than one, the biplane was a popular configuration.**

Fighter aircraft technology

When Orville and Wilbur Wright built their pioneering Wright Flyer in 1903, they used wood as the main material for wings and fuselage, braced by wires for added strength. By the end of World War II, most fighters were all-metal and flew at speeds the Wrights could have only dreamed of. The Wright Flyer was a biplane and a pusher aircraft, that is the propeller was used to push from behind rather than pull from the front as in later tractor aircraft.

The pusher arrangement was retained for some early fighters, in the days before the invention of interrupter gear, so that a forward-firing gun could be used with no propeller, which had tended to get in the way of the bullets. With no propeller in the way, the front seat was given to the gunner/observer while the pilot occupied the rear seat. The pusher arrangement was ultimately unsuitable for higher-performance fighters and dangerous – in the event of a nose-down crash, the engine and associated fuel tended to land on top of the two-man crew. The tractor configuration therefore became the norm for fighters and other aircraft.

The Wrights' aircraft's roll was controlled by wing warping, that is, bracing wires were pulled to twist the wing's outer sections. When World War I broke out, most aircraft designers were favouring the conventional tailplane and fin arrangement using trailing edge ailerons to effect roll in place of the limited wing warping.

As engine technology improved and speeds increased, drag on early aircraft became an issue and aircraft frames were increasingly covered and enclosed with taut fabric for streamlining. This technique was used into the mid-1930s, but by the time of World War II most new fighter aircraft were of all-metal "monocoque" construction. Whereas early fabric-covered fighters got their structural strength from taut metal bracing wires, the metal skin of the monocoque fuselage and ultimately wings and tail, welded or riveted to a light metal interior framework provided an incredibly strong construction.

The Wrights chose a biplane configuration for their Flyer and this form was used in most early World War I fighters as two pairs of wings generated much more lift than a monoplane. A series of pre-World War I accidents had led Britain's government to ban the Royal Flying Corps from using the apparently unstable and unsafe monoplane, and it was not until 1937 that the Royal Air Force deployed a monoplane fighter – the Hurricane. The Hawker Hurricane was an interesting aircraft and was a "crossover" design as it incorporated old and new aircraft construction techniques – it was a monoplane but its fuselage had a metal framework covered with wooden formers with a fabric covering.

As biplanes had succeeded in the first air combats, it was therefore inevitable that triplanes appeared, and in the cases of the Fokker Dr.I and the Sopwith Triplane were very successful.

LEFT: **Compare the complexity of this 1945 Grumman Tigercat cockpit with that of the 1914 Bristol Scout.** BELOW: **By the end of World War II, the wood and fabric fighter construction technique was obsolete.**

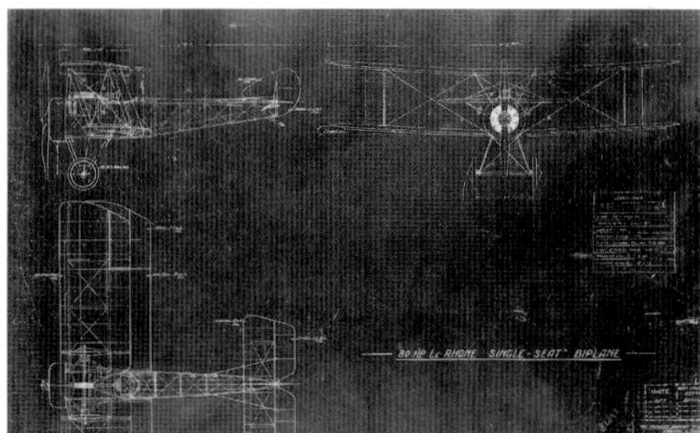

Sets of two or three wings had to be braced by fairly substantial wires and joined together with interplane struts which in themselves generated drag. A single wing of the same area would generate much less drag and being more aerodynamic would allow the aircraft to go that much faster.

Engine technology developed at an incredible pace in the first four decades of the 20th century. The 1914 Vickers F.B.5 with a top speed of 113kph/70mph was powered by a 100hp rotary engine, and less than three decades later the engine that powered the 697kph/433mph P-47 Thunderbolt was rated at 2535hp. Rotary engines, the principal combat aircraft engine when war broke out, reached their developmental peak by the end of World War I. Although relatively small and light, power output of the rotary dropped off with increased altitude.

By the end of World War I, air-cooled radials and in-line piston engines were clearly the way ahead. Both types of engine had much to commend them and both were developed to the maximum until the jet engine ultimately replaced them both. The importance of engine development in the evolution of fighters cannot be overemphasized. More powerful and efficient engines coupled with improved aerodynamics enabled fighters to fly higher and faster. Without a Merlin engine, would the Spitfire have been the fighter it became?

Although World War I had clearly demonstrated the military value of aircraft, in the years immediately after, fighter development was neglected – it was peacetime uses of aircraft that taxed the designers' ingenuity. However, speed competitions like the Schneider Trophy challenged designers to develop small, fast aircraft. With national pride at stake, these competitions generated huge amounts of worldwide interest. The Schneider Trophy races held annually from 1919 to 1931 did much to encourage innovation in engine and airframe design and showed that fuel science and super-charging were vital elements in the engine equation. Britain won the Schneider Trophy in 1931 with a Supermarine racing floatplane, a design that led directly to the legendary Spitfire.

ABOVE: **A Royal Air Force Spitfire. By 1945, piston engine technology had effectively reached its evolutionary limit.**

But what use is an engine without a good propeller? This vital but often overlooked element of the fighter aircraft "package" was itself dramatically improved between World War I and 1945. World War I fighters had two blades but late mark Spitfires had five-blade examples. As a propeller spins it generates thrust in the same way a wing develops lift. Early propellers were fixed pitch but in the late 1930s variable-pitch propellers were introduced so the pilot could mechanically adjust the propeller blades' angle for maximum efficiency at different speeds.

Towards the end of World War II, German and British jet-powered aircraft appeared and showed aircraft designers around the world the way ahead. The Messerschmitt Me262 could reach speeds of 870kph/540mph compared to the P-51 Mustang's top speed of 703kph/437mph. Designers knew that these early jet engines could take aircraft to speeds almost 25 per cent faster than the best piston-engined fighters in the world. The jet engine was the powerplant of the future.

Fighter armament

At the outbreak of World War I, aircraft armament was non-existent or ad hoc. The first fighters were armed with revolvers, rifles or shotguns carried by the pilots or observers but the importance of reliable hard-hitting armament was soon appreciated. Once weapons like the 7.7mm/0.303in Lewis machine-gun were proven, their use was then perfected. At first the guns were mounted on pivot pins or flexible mounts, aimed by the observers or pilots but they became truly effective once the guns were fixed to the aircraft and were synchronized to fire between the spinning propeller blades. To aim at a target, the pilot simply had to fly straight at it.

During World War I, two rifle-calibre machine-guns were usually enough to inflict serious damage on canvas-covered mainly wooden aircraft. By the mid-1930s this was clearly inadequate to destroy the larger, metal bombers coming off the drawing boards at the time. Consequently, more and bigger guns were used to arm fighter aircraft but where was the best location for them? Guns synchronized to fire through the propeller arc usually experienced a 10 per cent reduction in the rate of fire, and the number of guns that could be clustered around an engine was physically limited. The other option was to mount the guns in the wings – a far cry from the early days of air fighting when the gun's breech had to be within reach of the pilot so he could free jammed bullets. The down side of the wing-mounted gun, especially as wings became thinner, was the limited amounts of ammunition that could be physically fitted in the wing.

Most British World War I fighters were armed with 7.7mm/0.303in Vickers machine-guns and these remained the standard British armament until the mid-1930s when the Browning 7.7mm/0.303in was adopted. The Browning could fire 1100–1200 rounds per minute compared to the 750rpm of the Lewis. The muzzle velocity of the Browning was also greater than that of the Vickers – 811m/2660ft per second compared to 683m/2240ft per second. These performance figures are important because in most combats, pilots only have time for perhaps a second's burst as an enemy aircraft flashes by.

BELOW: **The synchronizing of fighter aircraft guns eased aiming for the pilots and thus improved the effectiveness of the early fighters.**

TOP LEFT: **Rearming an RAF Hurricane – two of the aircraft's four hard-hitting wing-mounted 20mm/0.78in cannon.** ABOVE: **Preparing to load the guns in USAAF P-51 Mustangs.**

During World War I, experiments had been carried out to see if large calibre weapons (cannon) firing explosive ammunition could destroy enemy aircraft. Early British tests found that the recoil of these comparatively large weapons was enough to stop a slow-moving firing aircraft in flight, let alone inflict damage on an enemy. French development work was more successful and a 37mm/1.45in cannon was used in combat by French aces Guynemer and Fonck, both of whom destroyed German aircraft with the weapon. Germany's World War I Becker cannon was later used as the basis for the early 1930s French Hispano-Suiza cannon that became the hugely successful Type 404 Moteur Canon.

In the mid-1930s Britain was behind the other major air forces in the procurement of cannon armament for fighter aircraft so it eventually licence-built the French Hispano-Suiza cannon.

When the legendary Spitfire first went to war its original armament was eight 7.7mm/0.303in Browning machine-guns but as the German Luftwaffe provided their aircraft with more armour and self-sealing fuel tanks it was apparent that the Spitfire's eight machine-guns were not adequate to inflict enough damage on enemy aircraft. Some Spitfire pilots were amazed to learn that enemy bombers claimed as "probably destroyed" had managed to limp home having suffered perhaps over 100 hits from 7.7mm/0.303in ammunition rounds. The Germans' ingenious self-sealing tanks, made of lightweight metal coated with layers of vulcanized and non-vulcanized rubber, must have saved many such aircraft from becoming airborne infernos. When the fuel tank was punctured by a bullet or shrapnel, the leaking fuel reacted with the non-vulcanized layer making it swell thereby plugging the hole. In spite of this, a hit from an exploding cannon round would have caused irreparable damage.

Aircraft like the early Hurricane with its eight machine-guns could unleash 160 bullets per second on a target whereas a 20mm/0.78in cannon carried by a Messerschmitt Bf109 could fire five shells per second – quantity versus destructive capability. The best solution was a compromise and so later Spitfires and Hurricanes carried a combined machine-gun/ cannon armament.

During World War I, pilots had aimed their guns using a ring bead sight but that kept them too focused on the target, unable to see what else was going on in the sky ahead. In the mid-1930s the electric reflector sight was introduced and was a simplistic forerunner of today's Head-Up Display. A bright circle of light with an aiming dot in the centre was projected on to a small glass screen in front of the pilot. As the image was focused on infinity, it also allowed the pilot to be aware of what else was in the sky ahead.

Although the machine-gun and cannon were the most significant air-to-air weapons in the period, unguided rockets were highly developed by the end of World War II. Soviet fighters had in fact been experimentally armed with bomber-destroying 82mm/3.23in unguided rockets in the late 1930s. This Russian rocket was typical of most unguided rockets, having impact-fused explosive warheads that could inflict major damage on a bomber. During World War II, Germany was equally advanced in the development of unguided missiles and was eager to produce any means of knocking enemy bombers from the sky. The Luftwaffe initially used adapted surface-to-surface 21cm/8.27in rockets with 10.22kg/22.5lb high-explosive warheads detonated by a timed fuse. By the end of the war, Luftwaffe fighters were routinely armed with up to 24 unguided air-to-air rockets which, fired as a salvo, represented a deadly threat to Allied bombers. More impressive was the crude but effective radar-linked fire control computer that tracked an enemy aircraft and then launched an unguided missile at optimum range. Luckily for the Allies, Germany's comprehensive guided missile programme did not result in production weapons before the war's end.

LEFT: **In World War I, formal uniforms were the normal flying dress, however impractical they were.**
BELOW: **In winter conditions and as aircraft ceilings increased, thick flying suits were introduced on both sides during World War I.**

Pilot equipment

What kind of equipment would there have been at the early fighter pilot's disposal?

Early cockpits had very few instruments – an airspeed indicator, altimeter, fuel and oil pressure gauges and little else. As fighters were able to climb higher and higher, so the aircrew had to wear more and more clothes to counter the effect of the bitter cold. A pilot's efficiency also suffers above heights of 3050m/10,000ft and pressurized oxygen is required above 5,500m/18,000ft or they will ultimately pass out. Face masks were developed to provide oxygen under these conditions and continue to be used today. Cockpit heating was not much use if the pilot's "office" was open to the elements but it did make a difference when enclosed cockpits were introduced.

Before World War I, aircraft had carried radio receivers and transmitters only for experimental purposes – the first use of radio between an aircraft and the ground was in the USA in 1910. Before the days of transistors, those early radios were large heavy pieces of equipment weighing up to 114kg/250lb and as weight was a crucial factor in early aircraft, they were just not practical. When radios were installed they were normally only capable of receiving or sending Morse code signals. The other complication was that due to the wavelengths in use at the time, a trailing aerial of 91m/300ft length had to be used. Improved technology was required to make radio more practical and by the mid-1930s, relatively clear speech exchanges over the air were becoming the norm. Leather flying helmets were produced with earpieces stitched in, while the oxygen mask also had a built-in microphone.

On March 1, 1912 Captain Albert Berry of the United States made the first parachute jump from an aircraft, and from the start of World War I observation balloon crews were equipped with parachutes. The life-saving devices were not, however,

LEFT: **By the end of World War II more practical flying clothing was the norm, as were the parachutes denied to pioneer fighter pilots.** BELOW: **This Spitfire pilot sports the standard RAF oxygen mask with in-built microphone fixed to his helmet, which also features in-built headphones.** BOTTOM: **The ultimate emergency exit. This pilot leaves his stricken aircraft and prepares to open his 'chute.**

issued to aircrew and this led to many unnecessary deaths on both sides. Early 'chutes were heavy and bulky and would have added greatly to the overall weight of an aircraft. There was also a ludicrous belief among British military leaders that parachutes would undermine a pilot's fighting spirit and that they would "take to the silk" when faced with danger.

By the last year of World War I, however, aircraft performance and better parachute design made the parachute a more practical piece of equipment. Germany had led the way and issued parachutes to its crews in the summer of 1918. The first time a pilot used a parachute as a means of escape and survived was on August 22, 1918 – Lt Frigyes Hefty of the Austro-Hungarian Air Corps left his burning fighter after a dogfight with Italian aircraft, landed safely and lived to tell the tale.

As the higher speed jet fighters entered service towards the end of World War II, parachutes were found to be unsuitable for emergency escape. The high speed airflow made it very difficult and dangerous to bail out in the traditional manner. In the same way that they had led the way with parachutes, the Germans pioneered the use of what came to be known as "ejection seats" that propelled the pilot clear of their aircraft's tail, usually approaching very rapidly from the rear. A Heinkel He219A-0 was experimentally fitted with compressed air ejection seats for both crew, believed to be the first of their kind in service. The Heinkel 280 jet prototype's seat was also fired with compressed air, as opposed to the explosive charges in use today. In January 1942, during a test flight of the Heinkel jet, the pilot lost control of the aircraft and successfully ejected. The pilot, Flugkapitan Otto Schenk, was the first of thousands of aircrew to have their lives saved by ejection seats.

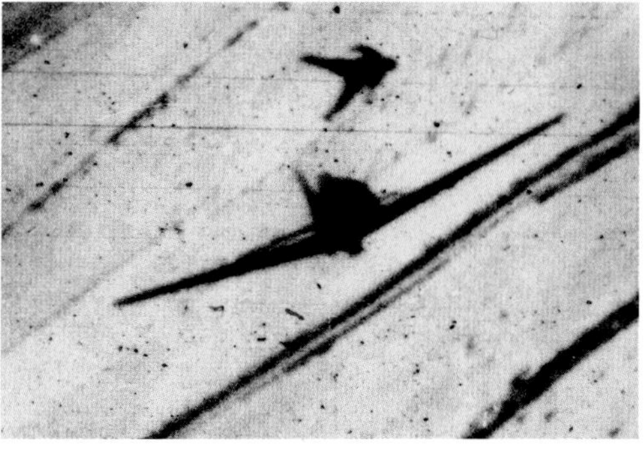

Blitzkrieg fighters

When Germany invaded Poland on September 1, 1939, precipitating World War II, a Blitzkrieg (lightning war) was unleashed on the ill-prepared Poles. The Blitzkrieg strategy was devised to create psychological shock and chaos in enemy forces through the use of surprise, speed and superiority. Proven by the Germans during the Spanish Civil War in 1938, the Blitzkrieg against Poland saw totally co-ordinated air (fighters and bombers) and land forces paralyse Poland's capacity to defend.

The best fighter aircraft in the Polish inventory was the P.Z.L. P.11 – with a top speed of 390kph/242mph the P.11 was still no match for the German Messerschmitt Bf109E that could fly over 177kph/110mph faster than the Polish fighter.

ABOVE: **The Messerschmitt Bf109, one of the all-time great fighter aircraft, was at the forefront of the Blitzkrieg, blasting ill-prepared opposition from the air.** BELOW: **By the time the Luftwaffe reached France, it met more effective fighters – the Dewoitine D.520s.**

That said, the Polish P.11 pilots made the most of their outmoded machines. Some sources claim that 114 of the P.11s were destroyed in the air battles that raged at the time of the invasion – although the defence of Poland failed, the P.11s did claim 126 Luftwaffe aircraft in the process.

The Luftwaffe deployed 200 Bf109E fighters and fighter-bombers for the invasion of Poland and the more manoeuvrable Bf109 was also better armed than the P.11 and Poland's even more antiquated P.7 fighters. The P.11s were however very nimble and not to be taken lightly, a mistake made by a number of Luftwaffe twin-engine fighter crews.

The Polish air defence ultimately failed partly because of the inflexible military structure of the Polish armed forces. Many fighter and bomber units were assigned to different armies tasked with defending different parts of the country and so there was no co-ordinated fighter response to the armadas of German bombers. A very significant element of the Polish fighter force was the Pursuit Brigade solely tasked with the defence of Warsaw.

The Nazi Propaganda Ministry had claimed that the Polish Air Force had been destroyed on the ground in the first day of battle but this was far from the truth. A formation of Heinkel He111 bombers trying to attack an airfield near Warsaw, was mauled and six were destroyed, the first falling to P.11 pilot Lt Aleksander Gabszwicz. On the afternoon of September 1, 1939, He111 bombers again headed for Warsaw, escorted by Bf109s and Bf110s. The air combats that followed after defending P.11 fighters were scrambled saw six German bombers shot down for the loss of five Polish fighters. So committed were the Polish defenders that one pilot rammed a Bf109 and baled out. The Polish defenders had prevented the Luftwaffe from dropping a single bomb on Warsaw.

The fighters attached to the armies saw much action and accounted for many German aircraft. In the first six days of war, army units claimed 63 Luftwaffe aircraft while the Pursuit Brigade claimed 42. From September 8, as the Germans pushed through and the Polish forces fell back towards Warsaw, the Poles' ability to defend themselves in a concerted manner was severely undermined. As the Polish infrastructure was dismantled by the Blitzkrieg, and starved of fuel, their fighter forces dissolved into chaos. On September 17, Soviet forces, acting in concert with Germany, also crossed into Poland, sealing the fate of the beleaguered nation.

The P.11s and P.7s continued to fight as they could until being ordered by General Rayski, Polish Commander-in-Chief, to evacuate to Romania. Many desperate and courageous Polish pilots had continued to attack large Luftwaffe formations on what were ultimately suicide missions. A number of Polish pilots escaped so they could continue to fight Germany from friendly countries. Some enlisted in the French Air Force and after the Fall of France made their way to Britain to join RAF Fighter Command.

Poland had fallen to the might of the Nazi war machine with Luftwaffe fighters playing a vital role in neutralizing resistance in the air. Blitzkrieg tactics were subsequently employed in the German invasions of Belgium, the Netherlands and France in 1940.

TOP: **German nightfighters, primarily developed to counter the RAF night-time bombing offensive, gave the Luftwaffe the ability to fight around the clock.** ABOVE: **The P.Z.L. P.11 fighters of Poland were not able to repulse the might of the Nazi Blitzkrieg.** LEFT: **Armadas of Heinkel He111 bombers, having honed their skills in Spain, carried the Blitzkrieg across Europe.**

The Battle of Britain

By June 1940 Belgium, Holland and France had fallen to German forces. The British Army withdrew from the Continent and the British Prime Minister, Winston Churchill, declared "the Battle of France is over; the Battle of Britain is about to begin". The so-called "phoney" war was over and the Third Reich's next objective was the subjugation of Britain. Churchill refused to consider peace on German terms and Hitler realized that he might have to invade Britain, which was protected from the German Army by the waters of the English Channel. On July 16, 1940 Hitler issued a directive ordering the preparation and execution of a plan to invade Britain. With Britain's large and powerful navy to contend with, an amphibious invasion of Britain would only be possible if the Luftwaffe could establish control of the air over the Channel and southern England. The Luftwaffe planned to destroy British air power in a wave of massive raids and clear the way for the invasion. As the Luftwaffe bombing attacks started in July 1940, Goering, leader of the German Air Force, thought that the Luftwaffe would easily beat the Royal Air Force, and so the German Army and Navy prepared to invade. Invasion barges were assembled in Channel ports.

ABOVE: **The Spitfire's well-documented role in the summer of 1940 earned it a place in world history.**

The forces deployed in the Battle of Britain were surprisingly small. The RAF had around 600 front-line fighters, mainly Spitfires and Hurricanes, to defend their country. The Germans had around 1300 bombers and dive bombers, and about 900 single-engined and 300 twin-engined fighters. Despite the importance of the campaign as a prelude to invasion, the Luftwaffe had no systematic or consistent plan of action. In contrast, RAF Fighter Command had prepared themselves for exactly the type of battle that took place. Britain's radar early warning, the most advanced operational system in the world, gave the RAF notice of where and when to direct their fighter forces to repel German raids, thus avoiding costly and misplaced standing patrols. This was a vital lesson which is as valid today as in 1940.

German bombers lacked the bomb-carrying capacity to mount truly strategic bombing raids against key military targets, and British radar largely prevented them from exploiting the element of surprise. Long-range Luftwaffe fighter cover was only partially available from German fighter aircraft, since the latter were operating at the limit of their flying range from bases across the English Channel.

Between July 10 and August 11, German air attacks were directed on ports and most importantly on fighter airfields to draw Fighter Command into combat. From August 12 to 23 the battle became more intense as the Luftwaffe launched Adlerangriff (Eagle Attack) hitting radar stations and trying to destroy Fighter Command in combat – inland airfields and communications centres were still heavily attacked. Up to September 6, RAF Fighter Command came close to defeat as the Germans intensified their efforts to destroy Fighter Command and obliterate British defences. Although British aircraft production increased and the Luftwaffe had lost more than 600 aircraft, RAF pilots were being killed more quickly than replacements could be trained. The RAF's effectiveness was further hampered by bombing damage done to the vital radar stations.

At the beginning of September the British retaliated by unexpectedly bombing Berlin, which so angered Hitler that he ordered the Luftwaffe to shift its attacks from Fighter Command installations to London and other cities. Although this led to many civilian casualties, it gave Fighter Command a short respite and time to regroup. In reality, the Luftwaffe's raids were somewhat formulaic which allowed Fighter Command to concentrate its fighter strength for the first time. By September 6, a huge German invasion fleet appeared to be ready to sail and British forces were put on "Alert No.2" meaning that an attack was probable in the next three days.

On September 15, the RAF's Spitfires and Hurricanes destroyed 185 German aircraft, showing the Luftwaffe that it could not gain air ascendancy over Britain. British fighters were simply shooting down German bombers faster than German industry could produce them. After the decisive RAF victories on September 15, the threat of invasion faded. The Battle of Britain was won, principally by the fighters of the Royal Air Force, and Hitler's invasion of Britain was postponed indefinitely.

ABOVE: **Messerschmitt Bf109s on patrol over the English Channel.** ABOVE RIGHT: **The fate of many Luftwaffe aircraft during the Battle.** RIGHT: **The Hawker Hurricane in fact destroyed more enemy aircraft than Spitfires, balloons and anti-aircraft defences combined. This photograph shows No.310 (Czechoslovakian) Squadron, Duxford 1940.**

Nightfighters

As early as World War I, German night bombing of Britain had been countered by defending fighters such as the Bristol Fighter and Sopwith Camel. Relying only on their eyesight and the hope of a bright moon, early nightfighter pilots did not constitute a practical deterrent and achieved only marginal success.

By World War II, defenders were assisted by ground radars, which could guide nightfighters to the general area where the enemy might be found, again by visual means. Truly effective night interception had to await the development of a radar small enough to be carried by the fighter itself. An airborne radar of this kind could aid in finding, stalking and bringing the nightfighter into firing range.

The USA, Germany, and Britain were all developing airborne radar early in World War II. Britain modified existing aircraft to fill the nightfighter gap. The Bristol Blenheim could not match the performance of day fighters like the German Bf109 so many became nightfighters, ultimately carrying the new and highly secret airborne radar. But even before the Blenheim IFs were equipped with radar, the RAF achieved some night-time victories – in June 1940 No.23 Squadron destroyed a Heinkel 111 bomber over Norfolk. However, the first radar interception came in late July 1940 when a Blenheim IF of the RAF's Fighter Interception Unit destroyed a German Dornier Do 17.

ABOVE: **The only specialized equipment carried by early nightfighters like the Bristol Fighter was the pilot's keen eyesight.** BELOW: **The Spitfire, with its narrow undercarriage track, was far from ideal for night operations.**

The Bristol Beaufighter was the world's first high-performance purpose-designed nightfighter and was a very advanced aircraft for its time. At the time of its combat début in 1940 the Beaufighter's devastating armament of four 20mm/0.78in cannon and six 7.7mm/0.303in machine-guns was the heaviest carried by any front-line aircraft. The closing months of 1940 saw the machine-guns fitted to the

LEFT: **The Northrop P-61 Black Widow – the first purpose-designed US nightfighter.** BELOW: **Only a handful of the Focke Wulf Ta154 dedicated nightfighters were ever built but indicated the realization that nightfighting was a specialized business.**

ABOVE: **A Junkers Ju 88 D-1 nightfighter.** RIGHT: **As aircraft were developed for nightfighting, so the cockpit began to accumulate new forms of equipment. The right seat position of this RAF Mosquito XIII nightfighter is dominated by the viewing apparatus of the AI Mk VIIIB radar.**

Beaufighters and, after a period of trial and error mastering the new radar with its range of 6.4km/4 miles, the aircraft's night victories began to increase.

Meanwhile, the United States directed its attentions to the interim Douglas P-70 and to the new Northrop P-61 Black Widow, the first US aircraft designed from the outset as a nightfighter. Lacking sufficient suitable US aircraft, USAAF units in Europe operated the British Beaufighter and later the Mosquito with good effect. In the Pacific, USAAF nightfighter squadrons operated the P-70 nightfighter version of the Douglas A-20 until P-61s could be delivered in 1944. By the end of World War II, the P-61 was the standard USAAF nightfighter and was in service with 15 of the 16 nightfighter squadrons operating in combat theatres worldwide.

German nightfighting began in the same way as the British – day fighters used in conjunction with a pilot's eyesight and searchlights on the ground below as the only means of seeing enemy aircraft in the dark. But by the summer of 1942 dedicated nightfighter groups were equipped with airborne radar. The RAF then began to use "Window", bundles of aluminium strips which, when dropped from the bombers, filled the sky with erroneous radar targets rendering German radar useless at a stroke. The Luftwaffe response in mid-1943 was the Wilde Sau nightfighters (Bf109 and Fw190) that relied on the illumination of enemy bombers by flares, searchlights or fires from below. Fighters guided from the ground by radar and helped by the ground lighting were then able to engage the enemy. German flak units were ordered to limit their fire to altitudes of 7000m/22,967ft so that the friendly nightfighters could operate in safety. Messerschmitt Bf110 and Junkers Ju 88 nightfighters equipped with radar and upward firing cannon did take a heavy toll of Allied bombers – literally hundreds were shot down.

The first uncertain steps in nightfighting led to the radar-equipped fighters of today, equally at home in day, bad weather and night conditions.

Fleet fighters

The year 1910 was a key year in the development of military air power. On November 14 that year a Curtiss biplane became the first ever to take-off from a ship. The aircraft flown by Eugene B. Ely flew from a 25.3m/83ft platform built over the bows of the US Navy cruiser USS *Birmingham*. Within two months Ely had succeeded in landing a Curtiss on a ship, this time the USS *Pennsylvania*. These feats were considered by many as nothing more than stunts but Ely had shown that aircraft actually did not need dry land from which to operate. By combining one of man's oldest means of transport, the boat, with his newest, the aeroplane, a new means of waging war was born.

Britain's first deck take-off came on January 10, 1912, when the Royal Navy's Lt C.R. Samson flew a Short biplane from staging erected over the gun turret of the cruiser HMS *Africa*. By 1915 Britain had two ships with 36.6m/120ft-long flying-off decks but they were far from operational. Flying-off platforms were, however, fitted to a handful of Royal Navy ships and a Sopwith Pup using the HMS *Yarmouth* flying platform was launched against and subsequently destroyed a German Zeppelin – this action is believed to have been the earliest use of a "carrier-borne" fighter for air defence.

The first significant use of carrier-borne air power came in the 1931–2 war between China and Japan. In January 1932, carrier-borne aircraft operated in support of Japanese land forces in action near Shanghai. It was not, however, until World War II that aircraft carriers and fighters came into their own.

TOP: **Three thoroughbred Grumman fighters – the Hellcat (foreground), Bearcat and Wildcat (rear).** ABOVE: **Early fleet fighter – a Sopwith 1½ Strutter takes off from the deck of HMS *Argus*.**

The carrier was vital in the World War II Japanese campaigns in the Pacific and enabled them to project power over vast distances. Carriers were able to make or break campaigns by providing strike aircraft and air cover for other ships, convoys and assault ships, making their protection vital. Each carrier had fighter aircraft to defend the ships and carriers from air attack. The US Navy developed defensive fighter "nets" over carrier groups to protect them from enemy aircraft by a combination of radar early-warning and standing patrols of fighters, some up to 64km/40 miles away from the carrier. A carrier that could be protected from air attack was a massive strategic asset in any theatre of war.

LEFT: **A typical scene from the flight deck of a Pacific theatre carrier.**

ABOVE: **Martlet/Wildcats prepare for take-off from the deck of a Royal Navy carrier.** RIGHT: **The deck of a wartime carrier was fraught with dangers. Here a US Navy Hellcat burns while another, wings folded, awaits orders.**

While Britain at first had second-rate or obsolete aircraft deployed as carrier-borne fighters, other nations developed high-performance hard-hitting fighters designed from the outset as carrier aircraft. One of the first true fighters deployed by the Royal Navy was the Sea Hurricane, the navalized version of the famous Battle of Britain fighter. RAF Hurricanes had flown on and off HMS *Glorious* during the Norwegian campaign in 1940 and shown that high-performance fighters could be operated from carriers. It was followed into Royal Navy service by the American-built Grumman Martlet (known as the Wildcat in the US Navy and later in the Royal Navy). The Wildcat proved itself almost immediately in its first carrier deployment on convoy protection in September 1941 by driving away or destroying enemy aircraft. Meanwhile the Sea Hurricanes soldiered on, tackling German torpedo aircraft while newer high-performance fighters were awaited from America.

World War II Japanese carrier-borne air power was formidable. Six aircraft carriers took part in the devastating December 1941 attack on Pearl Harbor which devastated the US Pacific Fleet. In this and other attacks, Japanese strike aircraft were only able to carry out their deadly missions because they were escorted by fighters such as the Mitsubishi Zero that fought with the defending fighters. The Zero was a formidable enemy to take on but its excellent manoeuvrability was achieved at the price of pilot safety. Every weight-saving measure was taken – there was no armour protecting the pilot and often there was not even a radio in the aircraft.

ABOVE: **Dramatic rocket-sled take-off by an early Sea Hurricane. Launched from a ship without a flight deck, the pilot had to find land or ditch.**

One carrier fighter in particular could be described as a war winner – the Grumman F6F Hellcat. Following its arrival in combat in August 1943, this tough fighter was able to turn the tables on the Zero and gave US Navy and Marine Corps pilots the upper hand until the end of World War II. Aircraft carriers had been shown to be as good as their defences, and in particular the fighters that protected them.

PETE McMANUS
HO
PETIE 3RD
U
CY

A–Z of World War Fighter Aircraft

1914–45

At the outbreak of World War I there were no fighter aircraft as such. Early aerial battles between aircraft with top speeds of around 135kph/84mph consisted of the pilots or observers shooting at their opposite number with pistols or hand-held rifles. Armed reconnaissance aircraft gave way to fighting scouts, the first true fighter aircraft. By the end of the war, one of the fastest fighters was the SPAD S.XIII with a top speed of 215kph/134mph. Compare this to the 660kph/410mph Gloster Meteor that flew into action late in World War II or the remarkable rocket-powered Messerschmitt Me163 Komet, which could reach 960kph/596mph.

These remarkable advances were made in only three decades. Piston engines were developed to their limits and jet engines, like those that equipped the Meteor, were produced as viable powerplants. Biplanes eventually gave way to monoplanes, and pilots came to be enclosed in heated cockpits as air fighting was forced higher and higher by attackers trying to evade defenders. But by the end of World War II, new aircraft designs and other technological advances were under development that would make the finest World War II fighters seem primitive by comparison.

LEFT: **A pair of North American P-51 Mustangs.**

LEFT: **The widely produced Albatros D.Va was an early example of fuselage streamlining.**
BELOW: **In early 1917 the D.I won air superiority for the Germans over the Western Front.**

Albatros D. Fighters – I, II, III, V, Va

The D series of Albatros fighters illustrates very well just how short-lived air superiority could be over the Western Front in World War I. As one side introduced a more effective type and achieved the upper hand, the enemy would develop a superior aircraft and very quickly redress the balance. The D.V was the last of a line of Albatros fighters that began with the D.I, developed into the D.II and then the D.III. As each version joined the fray it enjoyed only relatively short-lived success.

The Albatros D.I was introduced by the Germans to counter the Allied de Havilland and Nieuport fighting scouts, which had ended the "Fokker Scourge" of early 1916 and regained air superiority from the Germans. The D.I played a major role in swinging the pendulum back in favour of the Germans in early 1917. Apart from the fuselage, the D.I was built using components or building methods employed in the Albatros C series. The fighter's fuselage was elliptical in section and represented an advance in aerodynamic design over the earlier models.

The aircraft was powered by either a Benz Bz.III or a Mercedes D.III engine, which were then the most powerful engines fitted in a scout. This, coupled with the fact that the D.I was armed with two synchronized machine-guns, made it a hard-hitting fighter capable of climbing to 1000m/3280ft in six minutes – an impressive climb rate for the time. These factors made it attractive to the German "top guns" of the time, such as von Richthofen and Boelcke, who used the aircraft to regain air superiority for the Germans over the Western Front.

The D.II introduced a few fundamental improvements, including the lowering of the top wing so that the pilot could see over it and the aerodynamically improved installation of the radiator in the upper wing centre section. Climbing to 1000m/3280ft now took a mere five minutes.

The D.III was an improved version of the D.II, designed for better manoeuvrability. Changes to the wing set-up required the introduction of v-shaped struts between the upper and lower wings to improve rigidity. By late 1917 the D.III was in turn outclassed by the newer Allied fighters like the S.E.5 and was replaced by the D.V, the ultimate Albatros. The D.V had a wonderfully streamlined plywood-skinned fuselage and was produced in vast numbers. Over 1500 alone served on the Western Front, making up for any combat shortcomings by sheer weight of numbers. Heavy losses were experienced, not only as a result of enemy action but also to the Albatros's tendency to break up in flight, due to inherent structural weaknesses in the lower wing.

ABOVE: **The D.II had its upper wing lowered so that the pilot could see over the top.**

Albatros D.V

First flight: Spring 1917
Power: Mercedes 180hp DIIa six-cylinder in-line engine.
Armament: Two belt-fed fixed 7.92mm/0.31in Spandau machine-guns
Size: Wingspan – 9.05m/29ft 8in
Length – 7.33m/24ft 0.5in
Height – 2.7m/8ft 10.25in
Wing area – 21.28m²/229sq ft
Weights: Empty – 687kg/1511lb
Maximum loaded – 937kg/2061lb
Performance: Maximum speed – 187kph/116mph
Ceiling – 5700m/18,700ft
Range – 2 hours endurance
Climb – 1000m/3280ft in 4 minutes

LEFT: **An all-metal Siskin IIIA of No.49 Squadron Royal Air Force, pictured in 1929.**

Armstrong Whitworth Siskin IIIA

First flight: October 20, 1925
Power: Armstrong Siddeley Jaguar IV radial piston engine
Armament: Two synchronized 7.7mm/0.303in Vickers machine-guns in forward fuselage
Size: Wingspan – 10.11m/33ft 2in
Length – 7.72m/25ft 4in
Height – 3.1m/10ft 2in
Wing area – 27.22m^2/293sq ft
Weights: Empty – 935kg/2061lb
Maximum loaded – 1366kg/3012lb
Performance: Maximum speed – 251kph/156mph
Ceiling – 8230m/27,000ft
Range – 1 hour, 12 minutes at full throttle
Climb – 3050m/10,000ft in 6 minutes, 20 seconds

Armstrong Whitworth Siskin

This fighter had its origins in the Siddeley Deasy S.R.2 Siskin, produced by Armstrong Whitworth's parent company in 1919 and constructed mainly of wood. Britain's Air Ministry only wanted all-metal fighters and so the Siskin was redesigned. When the Siskin III joined No.41 Squadron at Northolt in May 1924 it became the first all-metal fighter in RAF service.

In total, 465 Siskin IIIs were produced, including some examples for export to Estonia and Canada. The improved Siskin IIIA, powered by a supercharged Armstrong Siddeley Jaguar IV engine, first flew in October 1925 and went on to equip eleven RAF squadrons from September 1926 – the newer model can be identified by the lack of the ventral fin beneath the tail.

Royal Air Force Siskin squadrons pioneered aerobatics in the service, some Siskins even being flown literally tied together at the famous Hendon Air Displays.

The last Siskin in RAF service was phased out in October 1932, although IIIAs supplied to the Royal Canadian Air Force soldiered on until replaced by Hawker Hurricanes in 1939.

LEFT: **The Avia 534, arguably the best fighter of its time.**

Avia 534

First flight: August 1933
Power: Hispano-Suiza 850hp HS 12Ydrs in-line piston engine
Armament: Four fixed 7.7mm/0.303in synchronized machine-guns in front fuselage plus underwing racks for six 20kg/44lb bombs
Size: Wingspan – 9.4m/30ft 10in
Length – 8.2m/26ft 10.75in Height – 3.1m/10ft 2in
Wing area – 23.56m^2/253.61sq ft
Weights: Empty – 1460kg/3219lb
Maximum loaded – 2120kg/4674lb
Performance: Maximum speed – 394kph/245mph
Ceiling – 10,600m/34,775ft
Range – 580km/360 miles
Climb – 900m/2953ft per minute

Avia B. 534-IV

This little-known fighter has been described as the finest fighter aircraft of its time, because of its combination of impressive armament, excellent handling and high speed. It was certainly the most important Czech aircraft of the inter-war years and was almost at the pinnacle of biplane fighter design, lacking only a retractable undercarriage. Construction of the 534 was an interesting combination of steel wings covered with fabric, and a fuselage of riveted and bolted steel tubes covered with metal panels or fabric. In April 1934 the second prototype set a Czech national speed record of 365.74kph/227.27mph.

Front-line Czech fighter units were equipped with over 300 of these fine aircraft during the Munich Crisis of September 1938, and after the German occupation of Czechoslovakia, Slovak Air Force units flew 534s against the Red Army in July 1941.

The Avia 534 interested the Luftwaffe sufficiently for it to form in late 1939, albeit briefly, a unit equipped solely with the captured Czech fighter. These robust and manoeuvrable fighters were later relegated to target towing duties.

LEFT: **The P-39, widely used by the Soviet Union.**

Bell P-39M Airacobra

First flight: April 6, 1938
Power: Allison 1200hp V-1710-83 in-line piston engine
Armament: One 37mm/1.46in T9 cannon, two 12.7mm/0.5in machine-guns and four 7.62mm/0.3in machine-guns
Size: Wingspan – 10.36m/34ft
Length – 9.19m/30ft 2in Height – 3.61m/11ft 10in
Wing area – 19.79m²/213sq ft
Weights: Empty – 2545kg/5610lb
Maximum take-off – 3810kg/8400lb
Performance: Maximum speed – 621kph/386mph
Ceiling – 10,970m/36,000ft
Range – 1046km/650 miles
Climb – 4575m/15,000ft in 4 minutes, 30 seconds

Bell P-39 Airacobra

The P-39 was the first fighter with a tricycle undercarriage. The type was also unorthodox because its engine was installed behind the pilot, as it was armed with a large-calibre cannon that fired through the propeller hub. The aircraft had in fact been designed around the 37mm/1.46in weapon from the outset. Initially ordered for the French Air Force, the aircraft were instead supplied to Britain.

The P-39 entered USAAF service in February 1941, and in September the same year, No.601 Squadron became the first and only RAF unit to operate the type. During the aircraft's test programme, a decision was made to exclude the engine's turbocharger and the consequent relatively poor performance did not endear the P-39 to the RAF, who only used the type for ground attack missions between October and December 1941. The USAAF, however, did use the P-39 with some success in North Africa in a ground attack role and around 5000 were supplied to the USSR, where they were used for similar missions. From 1942–4 the P-39, together with the P-40, were the main front-line USAAF fighters in the Pacific theatre.

LEFT: **At first the F4B had no engine cowling, but later a ring cowling was added to improve streamlining. The F4B equipped both the US Navy and Marine Corps, while the P-12 variants were operated by the USAAC.**

Boeing F4B

First flight: June 25, 1928
Power: Pratt and Whitney 550hp R-1340-16 Wasp nine-cylinder radial engine
Armament: Two fixed forward-firing 7.62mm/0.3in machine-guns
Size: Wingspan – 9.14m/30ft
Length – 6.12m/20ft 1in
Height – 2.84m/9ft 4in
Wing area – 21.13m²/227.5sq ft
Weights: Empty – 1068kg/2354lb
Maximum loaded – 1638kg/3611lb
Performance: Maximum speed – 303kph/188mph
Ceiling – 8200m/26,900ft
Range – 595km/370 miles
Climb – 1525m/5000ft in 2 minutes, 42 seconds

Boeing F4B/P-12

Boeing developed the F4B as a private venture to possibly replace the US Navy's Boeing F2B and F3B. The new aircraft was smaller and lighter than its forerunners but retained the Wasp engine of the F3B and included some design changes that together resulted in improved performance. Accordingly the F4B was ordered in great quantities for the US Navy and, later, the US Army who gave it the designation P-12. Both the US Navy and Army utilized a host of different variants many of which served on into World War II. Brazil was the only major customer outside the USA. Total production reached 586.

Boeing P-26

The "Peashooter" as it was known, was an aircraft that spanned two eras. America's first all-metal fighter produced in quantity is also notable as it was the last to have a fixed undercarriage and open cockpit. Boeing first proposed the P-26 to the US Army in 1931 having designed it around the trusted Pratt and Whitney R-1340 radial engine. The first prototype was built and flown in only nine weeks, taking to the air for the first time in March 1932 at Wright Field. The P-26's top speed of 365kph/227mph may seem sedate by today's transonic standards but it represented an increase of over 20 per cent compared to the performance of the P-12 it replaced. The order placed by the US Army Air Corps (USAAC) in January 1933 was at the time the biggest ever for a US military aircraft.

By the time the P-26 joined the USAAC squadrons in early 1934, a number of refinements and improvements had been incorporated including strengthening of the pilot's headrest fairing. An early version of the aircraft had overturned after landing on soft ground, killing the pilot as the headrest collapsed. The Peashooter was popular with pilots as it was light and responsive, and it was the fastest USAAC fighter until 1938. It remained in service until as late as 1942.

Boeing widely exported the P-26, but the aircraft had a high landing speed for the time, around 117kph/73mph, which was found to be rather high for the rough airfields of foreign air forces. Split landing flaps were fitted to reduce the speed at the critical landing time. In September 1934 the first of ten examples sold to China arrived at Canton. Over the next year or so the Peashooters were in action against the invading Japanese on an almost daily basis and succeeded in destroying some of the enemy's aircraft in air combat. Ex-USAAC P-26s were also supplied to Guatemala where they comprised the Guatemalan Military Air Corps' first fighter unit and remained in service until 1955.

TOP: **The Peashooter was the fastest USAAC fighter aircraft until 1938, and the type remained in Guatemalan service until 1955.** ABOVE: **The agile P-26 was America's first mass-produced all-metal fighter.**

Boeing P-26A

First flight: March 20, 1932
Power: One Pratt and Whitney 500hp nine-cylinder air-cooled radial piston engine
Armament: Two synchronized forward-firing 7.62mm/0.3in machine-guns on sides of nose
Size: Wingspan – 8.52m/27ft 11.5in
Length – 7.26m/23ft 10in
Height – 3.17m/10.5ft
Wing area – 13.89m^2/149.5sq ft
Weights: Empty – 1031kg/2271lb
Maximum take-off – 1366kg/3012lb
Performance: Maximum speed – 365kph/227mph
Ceiling – 8350m/27,400ft
Range – 579km/360 miles
Climb – 719m/2360ft per minute

LEFT: **Defiants of No.264 Squadron, RAF.**

Boulton Paul Defiant Mk II

First flight: August 11, 1937
Power: Rolls-Royce 1280hp Merlin XX piston engine
Armament: Four 7.7mm/0.303in machine-guns in power-operated dorsal turret
Size: Wingspan – 11.99m/39ft 4in
Length – 10.77m/35ft 4in
Height – 3.45m/11ft 4in
Wing area – 23.23m²/250 sq ft
Weights: Empty – 2849kg/6282lb
Maximum loaded – 3821kg/8424lb
Performance: Maximum speed – 504kph/313mph
Ceiling – 9250m/30350ft
Range – 748km/465 miles
Climb – 580m/1900ft per minute

Boulton Paul Defiant

The Defiant was the RAF's first four-gun fighter in squadron service, making its first flight in August 1937. Tactically, the Defiants were a departure for two-seat fighters as all of their firepower was concentrated in the rear turret and no forward armament was carried. They went into action for the first time on May 12, 1940 and by the end of the month had destroyed 65 enemy aircraft over France. The success was partly due to the devastating fire-power that could be unleashed on any fighter that got on a Defiant's tail. The "honeymoon" was soon over. In dogfights the Defiant was no match for the Luftwaffe's best fighters and losses began to increase. With no front-firing guns, the Defiant was vulnerable to head-on attacks and in August 1940 they were withdrawn.

Defiants were then "recycled" as nightfighters and fitted with the new and highly secret Airborne Interception radar. Over the winter of 1940–1 the Defiant had more kills per interception than any other RAF type. At the height of their use, Defiant nightfighters equipped 13 RAF squadrons, and played a vital role in the night defence of Britain.

LEFT: **Buffaloes entered RAF service in 1940.**

Brewster F2A-3 Buffalo

First flight: December 1937
Power: Wright 1200hp R-1820-40 Cyclone radial piston engine
Armament: Four fixed forward-firing 12.7mm/0.5in machine-guns
Size: Wingspan – 10.67m/35ft
Length – 8.03m/26ft 4in Height – 3.68m/12ft 1in
Wing area – 19.41m²/208.9sq ft
Weights: Empty – 2146kg/4723lb
Maximum take-off – 3247kg/7159lb
Performance: Maximum speed – 517kph/321mph
Ceiling – 10,120m/33,200ft
Range – 1553km/965 miles
Climb – 935m/3070ft per minute

Brewster F2A Buffalo

The F2A was designed to meet a US Navy specification for a carrier-based monoplane and was awarded the contract, making it the Navy's first monoplane fighter. Of the 54 ordered only 11 made it into service, the rest being sold to Finland. Further contracts from the US Navy brought the F2A-2 and the more heavily armed and armoured F2A-3 into service. US Marine Corps aviators used the Buffalo to the best of their ability in the first Battle of Midway, when 13 out of 19 were destroyed.

Orders placed by Britain (where the F2A was named Buffalo by the RAF and was found to be inadequate for the war in Europe) and the Netherlands East Indies brought more Buffaloes to the war in the Far East, where they were out-classed by Japanese fighters. The aircraft's failure was due to its poor manoeuvrability, heavy weight and basic instability. In spite of this, by the time of the fall of Singapore in February 1942, RAF Buffaloes had destroyed 30 Japanese aircraft in the air.

Only in Finland did the Buffalo hold its own, when from mid-1941 until September 1944 it successfully opposed Soviet forces in the Russo-Finnish War.

Bristol Beaufighter

The Beaufighter was not designed to an official specification – the Bristol company simply proposed a versatile heavily armed aircraft that they thought the RAF needed. Britain's Air Ministry was impressed by the proposal and the devastating fire power this aircraft could unleash, realizing they had found the heavily armed long-range fighter missing from the RAF inventory. Using the major airframe elements of the Beaufort torpedo-bomber already in production, the two-seat Beaufighter was produced quickly and joined front-line squadrons at the height of the Battle of Britain in 1940, only 13 months after the prototype first flew.

The "Beau" was the world's first high-performance purpose-designed nightfighter and was a very advanced aircraft for its time. At the time of its combat début with the Fighter Interception Unit in 1940, the Beaufighter's armament of four 20mm/0.78in cannon and six 7.7mm/0.303in machine-guns was the heaviest carried by any front-line aircraft. Crews found the "Beau" to be quite fast and manoeuvrable and experienced Blenheim pilots were able to manage the aircraft's demanding take-off swing. When Beaufighters joined front-line Royal Air Force squadrons in early September 1940, most only carried their cannon armament – the much needed machine-guns were retained for the all-important Spitfires and Hurricanes, should a shortage have arisen. The closing months of 1940 saw machine-guns fitted to the Beaufighters and, after a period of trial and error mastering the new AI radar, the aircraft's night victories against the Luftwaffe began to increase.

Day fighter versions saw action in the Western Desert and Malta while RAF Coastal Command also used the "Beau" to great effect, particularly over the Bay of Biscay against Luftwaffe Junkers Ju 88s. Bomber and torpedo-carrying versions also saw wartime service with the RAF and after the war's end, Beaufighters served with Coastal Command and in the Far East until 1950 and as target towing aircraft until 1960.

TOP: **A Beaufighter of No.235 Squadron RAF.**
ABOVE: **Nicknamed "Whispering Death" by the Japanese, the Beaufighter was a robust aircraft well suited to hot and tropical conditions.**
LEFT: **A well-worn Beaufighter IIF.**

Bristol Beaufighter VIF

First flight: July 17, 1939
Power: Two Bristol 1,635hp Hercules VI 14-cylinder air-cooled sleeve valve radials
Armament: Four 20mm/0.78in cannon in nose, plus six 7.7mm/0.303in machine-guns in wings
Size: Wingspan – 17.65m/57ft 10in
Length 12.6m/41ft 8in
Height – 4.84m/15ft 10in
Wing area – 46.74m²/503sq ft
Weights: Empty – 6631kg/14,600lb
Maximum take-off – 9810kg/21,600lb
Performance: Maximum speed – 536kph/333mph
Ceiling – 8083m/26,500ft
Range – 2381km/1480 miles
Climb – 4575m/15,000ft in 7.8 minutes

Bristol Blenheim

The three-seat Bristol Blenheim first flew in 1935 and was a technological quantum leap among RAF aircraft at the time. With a top speed of around 428kph/266mph, the Blenheim bomber was considerably faster than the 290kph/180mph Hind biplane it replaced and it could outrun many contemporary fighters. The first Blenheim fighter, the IF, was proposed as a long-range fighter that could escort bombers over hostile territory and also carry out ground attack missions of its own. Around 200 Blenheims were modified for these fighter duties, additionally armed with a gun pack beneath the fuselage consisting of four machine-guns. The type had first entered service in December 1938 and by September 1939 there were 111 Blenheim fighters in use with the RAF. Unfortunately the Blenheim could not match the performance of aircraft such as the Messerschmitt Bf109 and so many became nightfighters, ultimately carrying the new and highly secret airborne radar.

Even before the IFs were equipped with radar they achieved some night-time victories – in June 1940 No.23 Squadron destroyed a Heinkel 111 bomber over Norfolk. The first ever radar interception came in late July when a Blenheim IF of Tangmere's Fighter Interception Unit destroyed a Dornier Do 17 near Brighton.

The pioneers of the Blenheim night-fighters were a flight of No.25 Squadron who were in fact the first unit in the world to operate radar-equipped night-fighters. But Blenheim fighters continued to operate in daylight too and as late as August 15, 1940, during the Battle of Britain, No.219 Squadron were in action against a German raid on north-east England. Between November 1939 and March 1940, RAF Coastal Command also operated IFs, providing top cover for shipping. The Mk IVF was again a long-range fighter version of the Mk IV bomber, carrying the same gun pack. Around 125 served with Coastal Command, providing shipping with air cover, as had the IF. In April 1940 a pilot of No.254 Squadron shot down a Heinkel 111 that posed a threat to British ships off the coast of Norway.

TOP: **This Blenheim, preserved and flown in the UK is a rare survivor.** ABOVE: **A Blenheim Mk IF of No.248 Squadron RAF – note the ventral gun pack beneath the rear of the cockpit area.**

Bristol Blenheim IF

First flight: April 12, 1935

Power: Two Bristol 840hp Mercury VIII nine-cylinder air-cooled radial engines

Armament: Four 7.7mm/0.303in Browning machine-guns in ventral gun pack, plus one Browning gun in port wing and one in gun turret

Size: Wingspan – 17.17m/56ft 4in
Length – 12.12m/39ft 9in Height – 3m/9ft 10in
Wing area – 43.57m^2/469sq ft

Weights: Empty – 3674kg/8100lb
Maximum take-off – 5670kg/12,500lb

Performance: Maximum speed – 458kph/285mph
Ceiling – 8315m/27,280ft
Range – 1810km/1125 miles
Climb – 4570m/15,000ft in 11 minutes, 30 seconds

LEFT: **The prototype Bulldog II, J9480. The Bulldog was an unequal span biplane with a metal frame and a fabric covering.** BELOW: **A Bulldog IIA, preserved at a UK aviation museum. The type was the standard RAF fighter for seven years.**

Bristol Bulldog II

First flight: May 17, 1927
Power: Bristol 440hp Jupiter VII radial piston engine
Armament: Two fixed forward-firing synchronized Vickers machine-guns
Size: Wingspan – 10.34m/33ft 11in
Length – 7.62m/25ft
Height – 3m/9ft 10in
Wing area – 28.47m²/306.6sq ft
Weights: Empty – 998kg/2200lb
Maximum loaded – 1583kg/3490lb
Performance: Maximum speed – 280kph/174mph
Ceiling – 8230m/27,000ft
Range – 443km/275 miles
Climb – 6096m/20,000ft in 14 minutes, 30 seconds

Bristol Bulldog

The Bulldog was designed in response to a 1926 Air Ministry specification for a single-seat day- or nightfighter armed with two Vickers machine-guns able to take on the bombers of the era. The Mk I was used for development and it was the Mk II that replaced the RAF's Siskins and Gamecocks and first entered RAF service with No.3 Squadron at Upavon in June 1929. The Bulldog's fuselage was all-metal with a fabric covering, and it had a shock-absorbing tail skid, as operations were still exclusively from grass strips. Innovations for the Bulldog included an oxygen supply for the pilot and a short-wave two-way radio.

By 1932 the Bulldog equipped ten RAF squadrons and it remained the service's standard fighter until 1936. The 312 Bulldogs that entered service comprised about 70 per cent of the UK's air defence capability.

The last RAF Bulldogs were phased out in 1937, being replaced by Gloster Gauntlets. Many were exported to other countries, including Australia, Denmark, Siam (now Thailand), Sweden, Estonia and Finland. A two-seat trainer version was also produced.

Bristol Fighter

The arrival of the Bristol F.2B Fighter, powered by the new Rolls-Royce Falcon engine, over the Western Front ultimately proved to be very bad news for the German opposition. The aircraft had two crew – a pilot and an observer gunner in the rear cockpit. Each could engage an enemy aircraft independently – the pilot with a fixed forward-firing machine-gun and the observer with a Lewis gun (or two if he was strong).

Designed by Capt. Frank Barnwell around the Falcon engine, the armament of the Bristol Fighter was integral to its design from the outset, crew visibility was excellent and they had an unobstructed field of fire. The April 5, 1917 combat début of the "Brisfit" at the Battle of Arras was, however, far from successful as the Royal Flying Corps pilots used the standard two-seater tactic of leaving the aircraft's defence with the observer. This tactical error, coupled with oil freezing, which rendered a number of observers' guns useless, led to the loss of four out of six Brisfits on their first mission. Within days, the British pilots began to use the aircraft's forward-firing Vickers gun to full effect and flew the F.2B as if it were a single-seat fighter – the aircraft became something to be feared. The Bristol Fighter was to become the best two-seat fighter of World War I. When the Royal Air Force was established on April 1, 1918 it was a Bristol Fighter that flew the first combat mission of Britain's newly formed independent air arm. It proved popular with pilots because it was fast, manoeuvrable, could dive faster than any other aircraft in the theatre and it could take a lot of punishment.

The Vickers machine-gun mounted on the Bristol Fighter's centreline was beneath the engine cowling. Its location required a "tunnel" to be provided for the gun through the upper fuel tank.

Post-war the type was used as an Army co-operation aircraft and a trainer. Production of the Bristol Fighter continued until 1927 and the RAF took delivery of its last Bristol Fighter in December 1926. Fourteen foreign air forces, including Canada, Greece and Mexico, also operated the type. Fifteen years after entering RFC service, the Brisfit was still serving with the RAF in Iraq and India, at which time they were replaced by Fairey Gordons. The Royal New Zealand Air Force continued to operate Bristol Fighters until 1938.

TOP: **The combat début of the Bristol Fighter in April 1917 was far from auspicious, with four out of six aircraft being lost on their first mission.** ABOVE: **When both crew members used their guns, the Brisfit was a formidable fighter to contend with.**

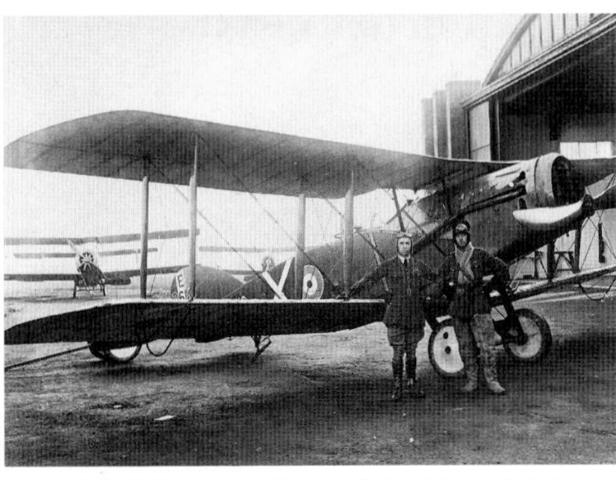

TOP: **The Bristol Fighter equipped RAF units in Turkey, India, Iraq, Palestine, Egypt and Syria.** ABOVE: **The Brisfit went on to become one of the best two-seat fighters of World War I.** BELOW: **Pilots and observers of No.22 Squadron of the newly formed Royal Air Force, pictured at Vert Galland on April 1, 1918.**

Bristol F.2B Fighter

First flight: September 9, 1916
Power: Rolls-Royce 275hp Falcon III in-line piston engine
Armament: One fixed forward-firing synchronized Vickers machine-gun and one or two "flexible" 7.7mm/0.303in Lewis guns in rear cockpit
Size: Wingspan – 11.96m/39ft 3in
Length – 7.87m/25ft 10in
Height – 2.97m/9ft 9in
Wing area – 37.63m^2/405 sq ft
Weights: Empty – 975kg/2150lb
Maximum loaded – 1474kg/3250lb
Performance: Maximum speed – 198kph/123mph
Ceiling – 5485m/18,000ft
Range – 3 hours endurance
Climb – 3048m/10,000ft in 11 minutes, 30 seconds

Bristol Scout

The Scout was derived from a pre-World War I racing aircraft and, had it been designed with armament from the outset, could have been a great fighter. Widely described as a very "clean" design, the Scout was certainly fast for its day and was used initially as a fast "scout", or reconnaissance aircraft. Soon after its appearance at the Front in February 1915, with its high performance, single-seat Scouts were allocated to two-seater squadrons as escorts. Armament on these first fighters varied widely at first, sometimes simply consisting of rifles bolted to the sides of the fuselage. In spite of this, on July 25, 1915 Captain L.G. Hawker used his Bristol Scout C to shoot down three enemy aircraft, themselves armed with machine-guns. For this action he was awarded the Victoria Cross, the first for aerial combat. At this point, Scouts equipped both the Royal Flying Corps and the Royal Naval Air Service, the latter using the Scout for anti-Zeppelin patrols armed with explosive "darts" thrown over the side.

When No.11 Squadron RFC was formed in February 1915 equipped with, among other types, Bristol Scouts, its sole purpose was the interception and destruction of enemy aircraft – it was one of the first true fighter squadrons. The British ace Albert Ball served with No.11 and liked to fly the Scout D which entered service in November 1915, equipped with a synchronized Vickers machine-gun. During one week in May 1916 Albert Ball used his Scout D, serial number 5326, to drive down four enemy aircraft and remove them from the war.

In all, around 370 Scouts were delivered. From mid-1916 they were gradually withdrawn from front-line duties to become training aircraft.

ABOVE: **5574 was a Scout D, the version that introduced a synchronized Vickers machine-gun.** BELOW: **A replica Scout D. Once the type was withdrawn from front-line duties the Scout was used for training purposes, and later a number were sold for civil use.**

Bristol Scout

First flight: February 23, 1914 (Scout A)
Power: Le Rhône 80hp rotary piston engine
Armament: One 7.7mm/0.303in Lewis machine-gun or local combinations of small arms
Size: Wingspan – 8.33m/27ft4in
Length 6.02m/19ft 9in
Height – 2.59m/8ft 6in
Wing area – 18.39m^2/198sq ft
Weights: Empty – 345kg/760lb
Maximum loaded – 567kg/1250lb
Performance: Maximum speed – 161kph/100mph
Ceiling – 4267m/14,000ft
Range – 2.5 hours endurance
Climb – 3050m/10,000ft in 18.5 minutes

LEFT: **The large and remarkable R.11.**

Caudron R.11

First flight: March 1917
Power: Two Hispano-Suiza 215hp 8Bba in-line piston engines
Armament: Five 7.7mm/0.303in Lewis machine-guns – two each in front and rear gunner positions, plus an additional "stinger" under the aircraft nose
Size: Wingspan – 17.92m/58ft 9.5in
Length – 11.22m/36ft 9.5in
Height – 2.8m/9ft 2.25in
Wing area – 54.25m^2/583.96sq ft
Weights: Empty – 1422kg/3135lb
Maximum take-off – 2167kg/4777lb
Performance: Maximum speed – 183kph/114mph
Ceiling – 5950m/19,520ft
Range – 3 hours endurance
Climb – 2000m/6560ft in 8 minutes, 10 seconds

Caudron R.11

The R.11 was designed in 1916 by René Caudron as a heavily armed reconnaissance-bomber, but the twin-engined biplane found its niche as a formidable escort fighter over the Western Front. Armed with five Lewis machine-guns, and fully aerobatic, the R.11 could escort French bombers to targets deep in enemy territory and dish out considerable punishment to German fighters that came near. The three-seat R.11, twice the size of other escort fighters in use at the time, built up an impressive tally of enemy aircraft kills.

A number of features make the R.11 stand out from many aircraft of the time. The engines were housed in streamlined nacelles to minimize drag, and both could be fed from one of two main fuel tanks as required. In late model R.11s the rear sections of the engine nacelles could be jettisoned, together with the auxiliary fuel tanks they contained. Another innovation was the provision of dual controls in the rear gunner's cockpit so that the gunner could take control if the pilot was incapacitated. The R.11 protected France until July 1922.

LEFT: **Developed from an aircraft which was itself derived from another, the Boomerang proved to be a very worthwhile fighter. The example pictured, sole survivor of the type, is preserved in Australia.**

Commonwealth Boomerang II

First flight: May 29, 1942
Power: Pratt & Whitney 1200hp R-1830-S3C4 Twin Wasp radial piston engine
Armament: Four 7.7mm/0.303in machine-guns and two 20mm/0.78in cannon in wings
Size: Wingspan – 10.97m/36ft
Length – 7.77m/25ft 6in
Height – 2.92m/9ft 7in
Wing area – 20.9m^2/225sq ft
Weights: Empty – 2437kg/5373lb
Maximum take-off – 3742kg/8249lb
Performance: Maximum speed – 491kph/305mph
Ceiling – 10,365m/34,000ft
Range – 2575km/1600 miles
Climb – 896m/2940ft per minute

Commonwealth Boomerang

The Boomerang was born of desperation and the sudden need in December 1941 to defend Australia from the Japanese. The aircraft was based on the Commonwealth Aircraft Corporation's earlier Wirraway which was in turn developed from the North American NA-16 trainer. The Wirraway's wing, undercarriage and tail were mated to a new fuselage and the resulting Boomerang prototype was produced in only three months. The Twin Wasp engine was considered too low powered for fighters elsewhere but the Boomerang design team used it to power their aircraft, which entered service in October 1942. This well-armed, tough and manoeuvrable aircraft first flew into action in April 1943 and proved to be an adversary to be reckoned with. As other fighter types became available the Boomerang was quickly replaced, having served in New Guinea and defended western and northern Australia in the country's time of need.

Curtiss P-36 Hawk

TOP: **A French H75, the export version of the P-36.** ABOVE: **One of the French H75s transferred to the RAF after the fall of France.**

Design work on the second family of Curtiss Hawks began in 1934 and led to the P-36 Hawk, which first flew in May 1935. It incorporated advanced features for the time, including an enclosed cockpit and retractable landing gear. The aircraft impressed the US Army Air Corps so much that Curtiss received an order for 210 machines, the largest peacetime order ever placed by the USAAC for a fighter. Deliveries began in April 1938 but by the time America entered World War II in December 1941, the aircraft was already thought to be obsolete, although some did see early action against the Japanese. P-36As were the main fighters defending Hawaii at the time of Pearl Harbor in December 1941.

Export versions of the P-36, the H75, were supplied to France where they saw limited action before the fall of France in 1940. One Armée de l'Air Hawk claimed the first German aircraft to fall to a French fighter in World War II. Most of the French Hawks were, however, transferred to the UK, where the Royal Air Force designated them "Mohawks". Some of the Hawks seized by the Germans were supplied by them to Finland after being used by the Luftwaffe as fighter trainers.

A further 100 Mohawks came to the UK direct from the USA between July and December 1940. Some were shipped to the Middle East and others were dispatched to India, where they entered service in December 1941. At one point, the fighter defence of the whole of north-east India was provided by just eight Mohawks. The last RAF unit to fly them was No.155 Squadron, which relinquished them in January 1944.

Hawks were also supplied to Norway (and the Free Norwegian Forces based in Canada), the Netherlands (diverted to the Netherlands East Indies) and Persia (now Iran). Vichy France, Finland, India and Peru also operated the type.

In 1937 a less sophisticated version of the P-36, the Hawk 75, was developed for export and supplied to China, Siam (now Thailand) and Argentina, where a further 20 were built. Chinese and Siamese 75s were used against the Japanese.

Curtiss P-36G Hawk

First flight: May 1935

Power: Wright 1200hp R-1820-G205A Cyclone piston radial engine

Armament: Four wing-mounted 7.62mm/0.3in machine-guns, plus two fuselage-mounted 12.7mm/0.5in machine-guns

Size: Wingspan – 11.28m/37ft
Length – 8.69m/28ft 6in
Height – 2.82m/9ft 3in
Wing area – 21.92m²/236sq ft

Weights: Empty – 2121kg/4675lb
Maximum loaded – 2667kg/5880lb

Performance: Maximum speed – 518kph/322mph
Ceiling – 9860m/32,350ft
Range – 1046km/650 miles
Climb – 4570m/15,000ft in 6 minutes

Curtiss P-40 Warhawk/Kittyhawk

The next version in the Hawk family tree was the P-40 Warhawk, which mainly differed from the Hawk by having an Allison liquid-cooled engine instead of the air-cooled Wright Cyclone radial. This model, more aerodynamically efficient than the Hawk due to the use of flush rivets, became the principal fighter of US Army Air Corps pursuit (fighter) squadrons. France had placed an order, which was instead sent to the UK after Germany invaded France. Britain had also ordered the new P-40s and designated them "Tomahawks". For the RAF, the Allison engine failed to provide the performance required for air combat in Europe in 1941 and RAF Tomahawks were used purely as low-level tactical reconnaissance aircraft. However, 100 British Tomahawk IIs were diverted to the American Volunteer Group operating in China, where they achieved many victories against Japanese aircraft.

The P-40D first flew in May 1941 and was a major improvement on previous models, with a new, more powerful Allison engine. The nose cross-section was reduced and the guns formerly carried in the nose were dropped. Main armament was now four 12.7mm/0.5in machine-guns in the wings and a rack could be added beneath the fuselage to carry a 227kg/500lb bomb. It was the British who ordered the P-40D and coined the name "Kittyhawk" for their version of the Curtiss fighter. (The name Kittyhawk is often mistakenly applied to the whole Warhawk range.) By now, however, the P-40 was way behind in contemporary fighter performance and it was not capable of holding its own against crack pilots. Nevertheless, the later P-40E model was also supplied to the American Volunteer Group in China, where it continued to achieve kills. Even in the Western Desert, where the RAF's Kittyhawks' fighter-bomber achievements are well known, the type had many victories in the air. Legendary British test pilot Neville Duke scored 12 air victories while flying Kittyhawks there, as well as the five kills he achieved whilst flying Tomahawks, also in the Western Desert.

Total production of the P-40 exceeded 16,800.

ABOVE: **This P-40, preserved in the USA, is painted as an aircraft of the American Volunteer Group.**
BELOW: **A fine wartime photograph of an RAF Kittyhawk in the Western Desert.**

P-40N/Kittyhawk IV

First flight: October 1938 (XP-40)
Power: Allison 1360hpV-1710-81 in-line piston engine
Armament: Six 12.7mm/0.5in machine-guns in wings and provision for one 227kg/500lb bomb under fuselage
Size: Wingspan – 11.42m/37ft 4in
Length – 10.2m/33ft 4in Height – 3.77m/12ft 4in
Wing area – 21.95m²/236sq ft
Weights: Empty – 2724kg/6000lb
Maximum loaded – 4018kg/8850lb
Performance: Maximum speed – 609kph/378mph
Ceiling – 11,630m/38,000ft
Range – 386km/240 miles
Climb – 4590m/15,000ft in 6 minutes, 42 seconds

LEFT: **A French Air Force D.500.**

Dewoitine D.500 series

The French D.500 may have been the most modern-looking fighter of its day but it was a transition design, bridging the gap between open-cockpit fabric-covered biplanes and the new all-metal monoplanes. The D.500, the prototype for the series, was made entirely of light alloy and first flew in 1932, attracting much overseas interest. It was a low wing monoplane with a fixed tailwheel. The D.501 was the first production version of a series that differed in engine and armament installation, resulting in a host of variants.

The ultimate version was the D.510 which, together with a few D.501s, was in widespread use in the French Air Force at the outbreak of World War II. Compared with the earlier models in the series, the D.510 had a more powerful engine and greater fuel capacity but with a top speed of 400kph/249mph, it would have been no match for Hitler's more modern and capable fighters.

It was transferred to French squadrons overseas before the German attack of May 1940. Some exported Dewoitines did battle in China until late 1941.

Dewoitine D.501

First flight: Early 1934
Power: Hispano-Suiza 690hp 12Xcrs in-line piston engine
Armament: One 20mm/0.78in Oerlikon cannon firing through propeller hub, plus two wing-mounted 7.55mm/0.295in machine-guns
Size: Wingspan – 12.09m/39ft 8.25in
Length – 7.56m/24ft 9.75in
Height – 2.7m/8ft 10.25in
Wing area – 16.5m²/177.61sq ft
Weights: Empty – 1287kg/2837lb
Maximum loaded – 1787kg/3940lb
Performance: Maximum speed – 335kph/208mph
Ceiling – 10,200m/33,465ft
Range – 870km/541 miles
Climb – 1000m/3280ft in 1 minute, 20 seconds

LEFT: **The long nose of the D.520 presented the pilot with a very poor view from the cockpit, so techniques used by RAF Spitfire pilots were employed – weave while taxiing and sideslip in to land.**

Dewoitine D.520

The D.520, with the look of a racing aircraft, was certainly the most capable fighter available to the French Armée de l'Air at the start of World War II. Production, in the face of initial official indifference was problematic, but they were rolling off the line at a healthy rate by the time France fell to the Germans. Some did reach French fighter units before the fall, and accounted for 147 German aircraft. Henschel 126s, Messerschmitt Bf109s and Bf110s, and Heinkel 111s all fell to the guns of the outnumbered D.520s.

Vichy forces used the D.520 extensively and with some success against Allied aircraft in the 1941 Syrian campaign and the North African landings of November 1942. D.520 production continued in Occupied France and these aircraft together with captured examples were supplied to Germany's allies, including Italy, Romania and Bulgaria.

The Luftwaffe itself was also quick to realize the D.520's potential as a fighter-trainer. These aircraft were later seized back by French forces after D-Day in 1944, had their German markings painted over, and were used against Germans in southern France. Post-war, the French Air Force operated D.520s until 1953.

Dewoitine D.520

First flight: October 2, 1938
Power: Hispano-Suiza 850hp 12Y-45 12-cylinder liquid-cooled piston engine
Armament: One 20mm/0.78in cannon firing through propeller hub, plus four 7.5mm/0.295in machine-guns in wings
Size: Wingspan – 10.2m/33ft 5.5in
Length – 8.76m/28ft 8.75in Height – 2.57m/8ft 5in
Wing area – 15.95m²/171.7sq ft
Weights: Empty – 2125kg/4685lb
Maximum take-off – 2790kg/6151lb
Performance: Maximum speed – 535kph/332mph
Ceiling – 10,250m/33,639ft
Range – 1540km/957 miles
Climb – 4000m/13,125ft in 5 minutes, 48 seconds

de Havilland/Airco DH.2

LEFT: **Four DH.2s of No.32 Squadron, Royal Flying Corps at Vert Galland, France, 1916.** BELOW: **A replica DH.2, showing the gun fixed in the front of the aircraft.** BOTTOM: **The DH.2 was vital to winning back control of the air in early 1916.**

In June 1914 Airco hired talented young designer Geoffrey de Havilland, later founder of the company that bore his name, to head their design department and the DH.2 was his second project for the company. The first had been the DH.1 two-seat reconnaissance fighter and the DH.2 was simply a smaller version of it for a one-man crew. The DH.2 used an air-cooled rotary engine instead of the DH.1's water-cooled in-line engine but kept the "pusher" configuration, with the propeller facing behind the aircraft. This was due to the fact that in early 1915 a means had not yet been perfected that would allow a gun to shoot forwards between the spinning blades of propeller blades.

The armament arrangement seems bizarre by today's standards, consisting of a Lewis gun which could be mounted on either side of the cockpit as the pilot wished. He did of course have to manhandle the gun (that weighed 8kg/17.5lb) to the other side if an enemy presented himself there, all while still trying to control the aircraft. The gun was later mounted at the front of the aircraft on the centre line and was normally used as a fixed weapon, aimed by aiming the aircraft itself.

Nevertheless the DH.2 was praised by its pilots for its responsiveness and excellent rate of climb, and the aircraft was certainly central to winning back control of the air over the Western Front in early 1916.

Around 450 were built, but the tide began to turn again, and the DH.2 was outclassed by the latest German fighters by late 1916. The type was eventually withdrawn from March 1917 but not before No.29 Squadron lost five out of six DH.2s in one engagement, with five of the new Albatros D.IIIs on December 20, 1916.

Airco DH.2

First flight: Spring 1915

Power: Gnome Monosoupape 100hp nine-cylinder rotary piston engine

Armament: One 7.7mm/0.303in Lewis machine-gun

Size: Wingspan – 8.61m/28ft 3in
Length – 7.68m/25ft 2.5in
Height – 2.91m/9ft 6.5in
Wing area – 23.13m^2/249sq ft

Weights: Empty – 428kg/943lb
Maximum take-off – 654kg/1441lb

Performance: Maximum speed – 150kph/93mph
Ceiling – 4265m/14,000ft
Range – 2 hours, 45 minutes endurance
Climb – 1830m/6000ft in 11 minutes

de Havilland Mosquito

The Mosquito was a true multi-role combat aircraft, which started life in late 1938 as an outline design for a bomber-reconnaissance aircraft that could fly so fast and high that no defensive armament was needed. The far-sighted design avoided the use of strategic materials, instead using wood for virtually the whole aircraft – this later led to the nickname the "Wooden Wonder". Even so, it was only after World War II began that Britain's Air Ministry seriously considered the proposal, and then with some caution, but in November 1940 the Mosquito first flew and convinced the sceptics that it was a remarkable aircraft. Priority production was ordered for the bomber version and meanwhile the photo-reconnaissance and fighter prototypes were prepared.

The Mosquito fighter prototype flew in May 1941 and was immediately developed as a nightfighter equipped with the latest secret Airborne Interception (AI) radar. It also differed from the bomber version by having strengthened wing spars for air combat and a flat bullet-proof windscreen.

Armed with four cannon in the floor beneath the nose and four machine-guns in the nose itself, the two-man Mosquito NF.II entered Fighter Command service in January 1942, gradually replacing the Beaufighter as the RAF's standard UK-based nightfighter. From December that year, No.23 Squadron's NF.IIs operated from Malta, and in the first few months of 1943 shot down 17 enemy aircraft. They were equally active in daylight and also flew train-busting missions over Italy, Sicily and North Africa, clearly demonstrating the versatility of the Mosquito as a fighter-bomber. The purely dayfighter version was shelved after one prototype, such was the effectiveness of the nightfighter and the later fighter-bomber versions.

TOP: **The bomber version of the Mosquito appeared first.** ABOVE: **The Mosquito sting – four 20mm/0.78in cannon below the cockpit. Later nightfighters had radomes like this NF.XIX, eliminating the external "antler" aerials.**

The radar carried by nightfighter Mosquitoes was constantly improved (Mks NF.XII, XIII and XVII) and the nose-mounted machine-guns were eventually deleted, leaving four cannon as the only armament. The crews became very adept at finding and destroying enemy aircraft under cover of darkness. On March 19, 1944 a Mk XVII of No.25 Squadron shot down three

ABOVE: **All Royal Australian Air Force Mosquitoes carried the A52 serial prefix denoting the aircraft type. DH Australia produced a total of 212 Mosquitoes during World War II.** BELOW: **Covered with matt black paint and with aerial arrays on the nose, the NF.II entered service in January 1942.**

Junkers Ju 188s on a single sortie over the Humber. Some of the XVIIs were equipped with a tail-mounted warning radar so that they could themselves avoid becoming the prey.

Fighter-bomber versions were also developed and the FB.Mk VI became the most widely used of all Mosquito fighters. This version was a day or night intruder, able ultimately to carry two 227kg/500lb bombs as well as the usual fighter armament. RAF Coastal Command were quick to see the potential of the type and soon began using the VI, armed with underwing rockets, as a maritime strike aircraft.

Mk VIs were equally at home defending the UK as nightfighters or flying deep into German airspace, wreaking havoc on their nightfighters. Mosquito VIs were also capable of catching and destroying the German V-1 flying bombs that rained down on parts of Britain from June 1944. In all, Mosquito fighters destroyed 428 V-1s, the first being claimed by Flight Lt J.G. Musgrove on the night of June 14–15.

In March 1944, a modified IV became the first British twin-engine aircraft to land on an aircraft carrier. This trial, on board HMS *Indefatigable*, proved the feasibility of the Sea Mosquito which, equipped with folding wings and a modified undercarriage, joined the Royal Navy in 1946.

The ultimate wartime Mosquito nightfighter was the NF.30 high-altitude version, which regularly escorted Royal Air Force bombers on missions over Germany. As one pilot later said, "The fact that we might have been there on their tail made some Luftwaffe pilots think twice before attacking our bomber boys".

Post-war, the Mosquito NF.36, fitted with American Mk 10 AI radar, appeared and an export version equipped with British AI radar was supplied to Yugoslavia. The NF.36 was the only all-weather fighter available to the RAF until 1951–2, when the nightfighter Meteors and Vampires entered service. It is hard to think of the Mosquito as a Cold War aircraft but it came to be so due to a technology deficit in the UK.

The last de Havilland Mosquito, out of a total production run of 7781 planes, was an NF.38, completed at Chester in November 1950.

de Havilland Mosquito NF.30

First flight: May 15, 1941 (fighter prototype)
Power: Two Rolls-Royce 1690hp Merlin 113/114 in-line piston engines
Armament: Four 20mm/0.78in cannon
Size: Wingspan – 16.5m/54ft 2in
Length – 13.57m/44ft 6in
Height – 3.81m/12ft 6in
Wing area – 42.19m^2/454sq ft
Weights: Empty – 6086kg/13,400lb
Maximum take-off – 9810kg/21,600lb
Performance: Maximum speed – 655kph/407mph
Ceiling – 11,590m/38,000ft
Range – 2091km/1300 miles
Climb – 869m/2850ft per minute

Fairey Firefly

From 1926 Britain's Fleet Air Arm deployed a series of fast two-seat fighter reconnaissance aircraft, and the Fairey Firefly continued the tradition, first flying in December 1941. It replaced the Fairey Fulmar as the Royal Navy's principal carrier-borne fighter from July 1943 and first saw action during attacks on the *Tirpitz* in July 1944. The Firefly's elliptical wings could be folded back manually for beneath-deck stowage and were hydraulically locked into the extended flying position.

Although the Griffon-engined Firefly Mk 1 was around 64kph/40mph faster than the Merlin-engined Fulmar, it was still slower than most contemporary fighters. The Firefly did however have better armament, in the form of four hard-hitting 20mm/0.78in cannons in place of the Fulmar's eight machine-guns. It also had great low-speed handling characteristics – vital for carrier-borne fighters.

Firefly nightfighter variants were developed early in production of the type and carried airborne interception radar in small wing-mounted radomes. The associated extra equipment affected the aircraft's centre of gravity and necessitated a lengthening of the fuselage by 45.7cm/18in. This version of the F.1, the N.F.2, was only produced in limited quantities because an alternative means of accommodating the radar equipment was developed that did not require major structural work. Radar was then being fitted as standard to Fireflies and the non-lengthened Firefly N.F.1 was the nightfighter version of the F.R.1, which was itself basically an F.1 fitted with radar. All Firefly nightfighters were equipped with exhaust dampers so that the glowing exhausts of the Griffon engine would not show up in darkness.

Although the Firefly was never a classic fighter, it excelled in the strike and armed reconnaissance role. The first Firefly air combat victory occurred on January 2, 1945 during a Fleet Air Arm attack on oil refineries in Sumatra, when a No.1770 Squadron aircraft shot down a Japanese "Oscar", a very capable dogfighter.

In the weeks immediately after VJ Day (September 2, 1945), Fleet Air Arm Fireflies carried out supply drops to POW camps on the Japanese mainland. Royal Navy Fireflies went on to see action in the Korean War and then, in 1954, in the ground-attack role in Malaya. Royal Netherlands Air Force Firefly AS4s were in action in Indonesia in early 1962.

ABOVE: **The early Fireflies had the radiator beneath the engine.** BELOW: **Later versions had wing leading edge radiators, changing the look of the aircraft.**

Fairey Firefly F.1

First flight: December 22, 1941
Power: Rolls-Royce 1990hp Griffon XII engine
Armament: Four 20mm/0.78in cannon in wings
Size: Wingspan – 13.56m/44ft 6in, spread
4.04m/13ft 3in, folded
Length – 11.46m/37ft 7in
Height – 4.14m/13ft 7in
Wing area – 30.48m²/328sq ft
Weights: Empty – 4423kg/9750lb
Maximum take-off – 6360kg/14,020lb
Performance: Maximum speed – 509kph/316mph
Ceiling – 8534m/28,000ft
Range – 2092km/1300 miles
Climb – 4575m/15,000ft in 9.6 minutes

Fiat CR.32

This biplane fighter, which first flew in 1933, has been described as one of the greatest ever aircraft in its class. The highly manoeuvrable all-metal aircraft proved itself during the Spanish Civil War, when around 380 flew in support of the Nationalist forces. It was more than a match for the Republicans' Polikarpov I-15 and I-16 monoplanes, and Spain built its own under licence as the Hispano Chirri. Other Fiat-built machines were supplied to China, Hungary and various South American countries. Even as late as 1940 the CR.32 was widely deployed by Italy's Regia Aeronautica. They were by then outclassed by contemporary fighters but some were modified as nightfighters and others soldiered on, some being used against British troops in Libya. Some of the Spanish Chirri models remained in service up to 1953 as aerobatic trainers.

LEFT: **The CR.30, proven in the Spanish Civil War.**

Fiat CR.32

First flight: April 28, 1933
Power: Fiat 600hp A.30 V-12 water-cooled in-line piston engine
Armament: Two synchronized 7.7mm/0.303in machine-guns
Size: Wingspan – 9.5m/31ft 2in
length, 7.45m/24ft 5.25in
Height – 2.63m/8ft 7.5in
Wing area – 22.1m²/237.89sq ft
Weights: Empty – 1325kg/2921lb
Maximum take-off – 1850kg/4079lb
Performance: Maximum speed – 375kph/233mph
Ceiling – 8800m/28,870ft
Range – 680km/422 miles
Climb – 907m/2000ft per minute

Fiat CR.42 Falco

Italy's air ministry, impressed by the performance of the CR.32 in the Spanish Civil War, believed the biplane fighter still had a place in modern air war. The Falco was really of another age by the time it entered service. With many air forces planning to equip with closed-cockpit metal monoplanes, the fixed-undercarriage Falco was virtually obsolete before it had flown. Nevertheless, the CR.42 was not only ordered for Italy's Regia Aeronautica but also for the air forces of Sweden, Belgium and Hungary. When Italy went to war in June 1940, Falcos flew as escorts on bombing missions over France. In late 1940 the biplane fighters were based in Belgium for Italian bomber attacks on Britain. This often forgotten aspect of the post-Battle of Britain period climaxed on November 11 when the only major Italian raid saw the Italian attackers severely mauled – Falcos were no match for Hurricanes.

LEFT: **This Falco is preserved in the UK by the Royal Air Force Museum.**

Fiat CR.42 Falco

First flight: May 23, 1938
Power: Fiat A.74 R1C 14-cylinder radial piston engine
Armament: Two fixed synchronized 12.7mm/0.5in machine-guns
Size: Wingspan – 9.7m/31ft 10in
Length – 8.27m/27ft 1.5in
Height – 3.59m/11ft 9.25in
Wing area – 22.4m²/241.12sq ft
Weights: Empty – 1782kg/3929lb
Maximum take-off – 2298kg/5060lb
Performance: Maximum speed – 430kph/267mph
Ceiling – 10,200m/33,465ft
Range – 775km/482 miles
Climb – 6000m/19,685ft in 8 minutes, 40 seconds

Fiat G.50 Freccia

The G.50 was the Regia Aeronautica's first all-metal retractable undercarriage monoplane fighter. Early models were combat-tested in the Spanish Civil War: pilots talked of its manoeuvrability and speed. The pilots did not, however, like the "greenhouse" cockpit canopy and, remarkably, the next 200 G.50s built had an open cockpit. About 120 were in service when Italy entered World War II and some were used on raids against France. G.50s also took part in the Italian Air Force raids on Britain in late 1940 and later participated in the Greek and Western Desert campaigns, sometimes in the fighter-bomber role. Only a handful were left in service at the time of the Italian armistice.

In 1939 Finland bought 35 Freccias (Arrow) and used them in action against the Soviet Union in the Russo-Finnish War between 1941 and 1944.

LEFT: **A Regia Aeronautica G.50.**

Fiat G.50 Freccia

First flight: February 26, 1937
Power: Fiat A.74 RC38 14-cylinder radial piston engine
Armament: Two synchronized 12.7mm/0.5in machine-guns
Size: Wingspan – 10.96m/35ft 11.5in
Length – 7.79m/25ft 6.75in
Height – 2.96m/9ft 8.5in
Wing area – 18.15m²/195.37sq ft
Weights: Empty – 1975kg/4354lb
Maximum take-off – 2415kg/5324lb
Performance: Maximum speed – 472kph/293mph
Ceiling – 9835m/32,265ft
Range – 670km/416 miles
Climb – 6000m/19,685 in 7 minutes, 30 seconds

Focke-Wulf Fw190

ABOVE: **The Fw190F was a fighter-bomber version. This example, captured by US forces, is seen awaiting evaluation at Freeman Field in the USA, September 1945.**

The Fw190, considered by many to be the finest Luftwaffe fighter of the war, was first flown in June 1939 and swiftly proved that single-seat fighters powered by air-cooled radials could still take on the best of the in-line engined fighters. When the Fw190 appeared in combat over France in September 1941 claiming three Spitfires, it proved to be bad news for the RAF whose Spitfire V had ruled the sky since its appearance in February 1941. The 190 was more manoeuvrable than the Spitfire V, except in its turning circle, and had a higher top speed. The Focke-Wulf fighter had a considerable period of dominance in the west and was only seriously challenged when the improved Spitfire IX appeared in quantity in the autumn of 1942.

In February 1942 the Fw190A had its combat début, providing air cover for the German battle-cruisers *Scharnhorst* and *Gneisenau* and the heavy cruiser *Prinz Eugen* as they tried to reach north German ports. In one engagement, 190s destroyed all six attacking Royal Navy Swordfish.

From 1942, the 190A began to appear in quantity on all major fronts and in the West served in both the air defence and fighter/bomber roles. Fw190s were in the thick of one of the fiercest air battles of World War II, over the British and Canadian landings at Dieppe on August 19, 1942. Fw190s were in action throughout the day, by the end of which their pilots had claimed a total of 97 RAF aircraft destroyed. One pilot alone, Josef Wurmheller, claimed seven Spitfires.

The A-model was constantly improved, carrying heavier armament and sometimes equipped with water-methanol or nitrous-oxide injection. Over 30 different variants appeared from the simple fighter to torpedo-carriers.

In the later war years, the Fw190 became the standard home defence fighter for Germany and was in constant action against the Allied bomber streams. On August 17, 1943 a USAAF bomber force was intercepted by over 300 Fw190 fighters who accounted for 60 American bombers destroyed and 100 damaged. Some of the 190s were specially equipped with 210mm/8.19in rockets used to blow the defensive formations apart, making the bombers easier targets for the conventionally armed Fw190s.

In June 1943 a dedicated Fw190 nightfighter unit was formed but the aircraft were not fitted with radar, instead relying on intercepting the bombers over targets where they might be illuminated by flares, searchlights or the light of the fires below. Over 200 RAF heavy bombers are believed to have been destroyed by these aircraft.

In 1943, the Luftwaffe was faced with an urgent need for fighters with better high-altitude performance to face not just the threat of Allied bombers but also the American B-29 that was known to be coming into service. The existing Fw190 was thought to be incapable of intercepting this new American bomber and so Focke-Wulf, under the leadership of Kurt Tank, undertook the development of a high altitude version of his Fw190 fighter to meet the threat.

The result was the long-nosed D model, or "Dora", and the first production version was the Fw190D-9, which attained production status in the early summer of 1944. The Fw190D

LEFT: **The versatile Fw190 was an excellent fighter-bomber. This example is shown carrying a bomb below its centre line.** BELOW: **The D model, or "Dora" was introduced to counter the anticipated threat of USAAF B-29s.**

BELOW RIGHT: **A captured Ta152H-1 in RAF markings. The Ta152 was an even longer-nosed derivative of the Fw190D.** BELOW: **This Fw190A-3 landed in the UK by mistake during June 1943, giving the Allies all the information they needed about the type.**

was the first production Fw190 fitted with a liquid-cooled engine and was a very good high-altitude interceptor, equal to the P-51D or Spitfire Mk XIV and without the altitude limitations of the Fw190A. Delivery of the Fw190D-9 began in August 1944 and the first Gruppe (group) to convert to the Dora-9 was 3/JG 54. Their first mission was to provide top cover for Me 262 jet fighters during take-off when they were at their most vulnerable. The general opinion of the Fw190D-9 pilots was that it was the finest Luftwaffe propeller fighter of the entire war and many considered it more than a match for the P-51 Mustang.

The D model was the stepping-stone to the high-flying Focke-Wulf Ta152 that saw service in limited numbers towards the end of the war.

Focke-Wulf 190D-9

First flight: June 1, 1939 (Fw190)

Power: Junkers 1776hp Jumo 213A-1 inverted V piston engine

Armament: Two 13mm/0.51in machine-guns, two 20mm/0.79in cannon plus one 500kg/1102lb bomb

Size: Wingspan – 10.5m/34ft 5.5in
Length – 10.2m/33ft 5.5in
Height – 3.35m/11ft
Wing area – 18.3m²/197sq ft

Weights: Empty – 3490kg/7694lb
Maximum take-off – 4848kg/10,670lb

Performance: Maximum speed – 685kph/426mph
Ceiling – 12,000m/39,370ft
Range – 835km/519 miles
Climb – 6000m/19,685ft in 7 minutes, 6 seconds

Fokker Eindecker

The Fokker E (Eindecker or monoplane) was significant because it was the first combat aircraft to be equipped with interrupter gear that allowed bullets from a fixed machine-gun to be fired safely between the spinning blades of a propeller. This gave the Eindecker pilots a significant advantage over their Allied adversaries, who still had to manoeuvre their aircraft into a firing position and then aim their moving guns manually. The interrupter gear synchronized the Eindecker's single gun with the propeller blades so that once the aircraft was pointed at a target, so was the gun.

The Eindecker, not a remarkable aircraft, was developed from the pre-war M.5 design and relied on "wing-warping" for lateral control, but the technical advantage of a single synchronized gun allowed its pilots to rack up a significant number of aerial victories, beginning on August 1, 1915, when the legendary German ace Max Immelmann achieved his and the Eindecker's first "kill". Over the following weeks Royal Flying Corps pilots were alarmed to come across these single-seat "fighters" that could fire along their own line of flight. This was the beginning of a period of German air supremacy over the Western Front that came to be known as the "Fokker Scourge". The Eindecker, with its innovative armament, gave pilots like Immelmann and Oswald Boelcke a string of victories that made them national heroes in their homeland and possibly the first well-known fighter aces.

In spite of this, for a number of reasons the Eindecker never reached its full potential as a weapon. German paranoia about the "secret" of the interrupter gear falling into British hands made them forbid the use of the Eindeckers over enemy territory. Also, the Eindeckers were only allocated as individual aircraft to fly escort for two-seater aircraft. Production problems meant that even though they were clearly very significant aircraft, there were less than a hundred in service by the end of 1915. Nevertheless, Eindecker pilots honed their tactics and eventually began to operate in fours, while a more organized ground control system had them vectored to airspace where enemy aircraft were known to be. The result was that by the end of 1915 a small number of Eindeckers had effectively removed the enemy's ability to carry out reconnaissance missions. Meanwhile two lone Eindeckers on the Eastern Front kept the Imperial Russian Air Service in their area at bay.

The tactical advantage enjoyed by the Fokker E series (later Es, the EII, III and IV had more powerful engines and/or an additional gun) came to an end, as Allied designers produced purpose-built fighters to counter the "Fokker Scourge" and Eindeckers were gradually replaced during 1916, but they are thought to have destroyed over 1000 Allied aircraft in their short time of supremacy.

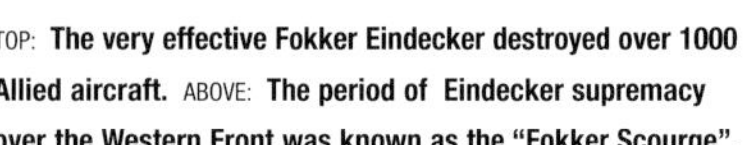

TOP: **The very effective Fokker Eindecker destroyed over 1000 Allied aircraft.** ABOVE: **The period of Eindecker supremacy over the Western Front was known as the "Fokker Scourge".**

Fokker Eindecker

First flight: 1913 (M.5)
Power: Oberursel 100hp U.I nine-cylinder rotary piston engine
Armament: One fixed forward-firing 7.92mm/0.31in machine-gun
Size: Wingspan – 9.5m/31ft 2.75in
Length – 7.2m/23ft 7.5in
Height – 2.4m/7ft 10.5in
Wing area – $16m^2$/172.23sq ft
Weight: Empty – 399kg/880lb
Maximum take-off – 610kg/1345lb
Performance: Maximum speed – 140kph/87mph
Ceiling – 3500m/11,480ft
Range – 1.5 hours endurance
Climb – 3000m/9845ft in 30 minutes

Fokker Dr.I Triplane

The Dr.I, chosen by the Germans to counter the threat posed by the British Sopwith Triplane, was rushed into production in 1917 and reached front-line units in October that year. Although extremely manoeuvrable the Dr.I (Dr. was short for Dreidecker or triplane) had an enormous amount of induced drag from its three wings and was consequently not as fast as most of the fighter aircraft then in front-line service. It was, however, extremely manoeuvrable and became the mount of some of Germany's finest World War I aces. The Dr.I will be forever linked with the "Red Baron", Manfred von Richthofen.

Lt Werner Voss scored ten victories flying a prototype Dr.I between September 3 and September 23, 1917 when he died in a dogfight with a Royal Flying Corps S.E.5a. Production models first joined Manfred von Richthofen's Jagdgeschwader (fighter squadron) 1 in mid-October but were grounded after a series of fatal crashes. Investigations found defective wing construction and the Dr.Is were back in action from the end of November only after all wings had been checked and if necessary rebuilt. Its career was, however, short-lived and production ceased in May 1918, at which time all remaining Dr.Is were withdrawn from the air defence of Germany. Although it was manoeuvrable, the Fokker was outclassed in many other ways and was really the last of the line of rotary-engined fighters. Richthofen, however, liked its agility and excellent climb rate and was flying his personal scarlet machine when he was shot down and killed in April 1918.

Lt Carl Jacobs was the highest scoring Imperial German Air Force Triplane pilot, credited with 41 victories.

ABOVE: Perhaps best known as the type made famous by the Red Baron, the Dr.I was one of the rotary-engined fighters. LEFT: The Fokker Triplane was introduced to counter the British Sopwith Triplane, which was very manoeuvrable.

Fokker Dr.I Triplane

First flight: June 1917
Power: Oberursel Ur.II nine-cylinder rotary piston engine
Armament: Two fixed forward-firing 7.92mm/0.31in machine-guns
Size: Wingspan – 7.2m/23ft 7.5in
Length – 5.77m/18ft 11.25in
Height – 2.95m/9ft 8.25in
Wing area – 18.7m²/201.29sq ft
Weights: Empty – 406kg/895lb
Maximum take-off – 585kg/1290lb
Performance: Maximum speed – 165kph/103mph
Ceiling – 6095m/20,000ft
Range – 1.5 hours endurance
Climb – 1000m/3280ft in 2 minutes, 54 seconds

Fokker D. VII

The D. VII followed the Dr.I into production at the Fokker factory and went on to become the most famous German fighting scout aircraft of World War I. Like the Dreidecker before it, the D. VII was largely designed by Fokker designer Reinhold Platz and shared a number of common components and features with it. The 160hp engine fitted to early D. VIIs was, however, a major step forward in terms of power and the first test flight was carried out by Manfred Richthofen. It first entered service in April 1918 with Jagdgeschwader 1, Richthofen's old unit, commanded by Hermann Goering after the "Red Baron's" death.

The D. VII was popular with its pilots, who described it as responsive and easy to fly. Pilots of this last World War I Fokker fighter achieved many aerial victories in a short period. Germany's first true naval fighter unit Marine-Feld-Geschwader was formed in May 1917 and it was this unit which on August 12, equipped with D. VIIs, shot down 19 British aircraft without loss to itself. The only Allied aircraft that could match the D. VII were the Sopwith Snipe and the SPAD S.XIII.

It is believed that over 1000 were built by the time of the Armistice in November 1918. It is interesting to note that one of the conditions of the Armistice Agreement was that "... especially all first-line D. VII aircraft" were to be handed over to the Allies, such was the regard for the Fokker fighter.

The Fokker company had been founded by Dutchman Anthony Fokker, who having had some of his designs rejected by Britain, among others, offered his services to the Central Powers. At the end of World War I, Fokker managed to smuggle some disassembled D. VIIs and components into Holland, where he went on manufacturing D. VIIs after the war. The Dutch Air Force continued to fly D. VIIs in the Netherlands East Indies until the late 1920s. Ex-German D. VIIs also served with many European air forces after the war.

TOP: **The Fokker D. VII was such a potent fighter that it was specifically mentioned in the Armistice Agreement.** ABOVE: **Oberleutnant Ernst Udet with his personal D. VII. His personal "LO" markings are just visible on the side of the fuselage.**

Fokker D. VII

First flight: January 1918
Power: BMW 185hp six-cylinder in-line piston engine
Armament: Two fixed forward-firing 7.92mm/0.3in machine-guns
Size: Wingspan – 8.9m/29ft 2.5in
Length – 6.95m/22ft 9.5in
Height – 2.75m/9ft 0.25in,
Wing area – 20.5m^2/220.67sq ft
Weights: Empty – 735kg/1620lb
Maximum take-off – 880kg/1940lb
Performance: Maximum speed – 200kph/124mph
Ceiling – 7000m/22,965ft
Range – 1.5 hours endurance
Climb – 5000m/16,405ft in 16 minutes

LEFT: **A D. XXI of the Finnish Air Force, 1941.**

Fokker D. XXI

First flight: March 27, 1936
Power: Bristol 830hp Mercury VIII nine-cylinder radial piston engine
Armament: Four 7.9mm/0.31in machine-guns, two in upper cowling and two in wings
Size: Wingspan – 11m/36ft 1in
Length – 8.2m/26ft 10.75in
Height – 2.95m/9ft 8in
Wing area – 16.2m²/174.38sq ft
Weights: Empty – 1450kg/3197lb
Maximum take-off – 2050kg/4519lb
Performance: Maximum speed – 460kph/286mph
Ceiling – 11,000m/36,090ft
Range – 950km/590 miles
Climb – 3000m/9842ft in 3 minutes, 30 seconds

Fokker D. XXI

Although the D. XXI was designed to meet a Netherlands East Indies Army Air Service requirement, it became the standard fighter for three European countries – Holland, Finland and Denmark. The first Dutch Air Force aircraft flew in mid-1938 and all were in service by early September 1938. The Dutch Air Force had 28 D. XXIs deployed when Germany invaded the Netherlands in May 1940. During the five days before Holland surrendered, the Fokker fighters were pitched against overwhelming odds, but on May 10 they destroyed 37 German Junkers 52 transports in one morning. The brave Dutch D. XXI pilots flew on until their ammunition ran out.

Finnish licence production ran from 1939 until 1944, and a number of these machines were modified to take the 825hp Pratt and Whitney Twin Wasp Junior or the Bristol Pegasus engines. Finnish aircraft also differed from the others by having all four guns mounted in the wings, and "snow shoes" for winter operations.

Denmark operated both Dutch-built and Danish licence-built D. XXIs, which saw action in World War II, opposing the German invaders in March 1940.

LEFT: **Royal Air Force Gauntlet Is. The type was replaced by Gladiators, Spitfires and Hurricanes from 1938, but soldiered on in RAF service overseas until late 1940.**

Gloster Gauntlet II

First flight: October 1934 (Gauntlet I)
Power: Bristol 640hp Mercury VIS nine-cylinder radial piston engine
Armament: Two fixed forward-firing 7.7mm/0.303in machine-guns
Size: Wingspan – 9.99m/32ft 9.5in
Length – 8.05m/26ft 5in
Height – 3.12m/10ft 3in
Wing area – 29.26m²/315sq ft
Weights: Empty – 1256kg/2770lb
Maximum take-off – 1801kg/3970lb
Performance: Maximum speed – 370kph/230mph
Ceiling – 10,210m/33,500ft
Range – 740km/460 miles
Climb – 701m/2300ft per minute

Gloster Gauntlet

The Gauntlet was the last open-cockpit biplane fighter with the RAF, entering service in 1935. It was the fastest single-seat fighter in service until 1937, when the Hurricane appeared, and served as a day- and nightfighter.

Gauntlets went on to equip 14 squadrons of RAF Fighter Command and remained a front-line aircraft in the UK until June 1939. However, the type soldiered on with No.6 Squadron in Palestine until April 1940 and a flight of four fought the Italians in East Africa during September-November 1940. On September 7 a Gauntlet downed an Italian Caproni Ca133 bomber.

In November 1937 it was a Gauntlet of No.32 Squadron that became the first fighter ever to carry out an interception under the direction of ground radar.

Seventeen Gauntlets were produced under licence in Denmark, and ex-RAF Gauntlets were supplied to the Royal Australian Air Force, Finland, Rhodesia and South Africa. The Finnish Gauntlets were fitted with ski landing gear.

Gloster Meteor

TOP: **A Meteor F.8, the only British jet type to see action in the Korean War.**
ABOVE: **Over 1000 Meteor F.8s were in service with the RAF between 1950 and 1955.**

The Gloster Meteor was the first jet aircraft in RAF squadron service and also the only Allied jet to see action in World War II. The Meteor beat Germany's Messerschmitt Me262 into squadron service and entered the history books by a matter of days to become the world's first operational jet fighter.

The Meteor was designed by George Carter, who began design work in 1940 and chose the twin-engine layout because of the poor thrust produced by the turbojets of the time. The first Meteor to be built was powered by two Frank Whittle-designed W2B turbojets, but the aircraft was only taxied as the engines failed to produce more than 454kg/1000lb of thrust. So when, on March 5, 1943 the first Meteor flew, it was powered by two Halford H1 engines, forerunners of the Goblin engine later used in the de Havilland Vampire, each providing 681kg/1500lb of thrust. Other prototypes soon took to the air, powered by different engines as the most reliable and efficient powerplant was sought. Development and manufacture of the Whittle-designed engine had passed to Rolls-Royce, who produced it as the 772kg/1700lb thrust W2B/23 Welland engine and it was two of these powerplants that took the fourth Meteor prototype into the air for the first time in June 1943. The Welland was subsequently chosen to power the production Meteor I.

The first RAF Meteor squadron was No.616, who received their first delivery of the futuristic fighters on July 12, 1944 and wasted no time in putting the Meteor to the test. The first sortie flown by a Meteor was not against manned aircraft but actually against the deadly V-1 flying bombs that began to rain down on Britain in 1944. Problems with the guns frustrated Britain's first jet pilots but on August 4 Flying Officer Dean succeeded in tipping a V-1 over in flight after his guns had jammed. By the end of the month, with gun problems resolved, No.616 had destroyed a total of 13 flying bombs. As the Allies pushed into Europe after D-Day, the next Meteors were readied for fighter v. fighter combat, possibly against the new twin-engined Me262 recently deployed by the Germans. In fact only one inconclusive encounter with Focke-Wulf Fw190s is recorded. As World War II came to an end, the Meteor F. Mk III was the standard version in service, with more

powerful Derwent engines and a sliding canopy. These aircraft remained in RAF service for some years after the war and formed the backbone of Fighter Command in the post-war years, retaining the standard wartime armament of four 20mm/0.78in Hispano cannon, carried on the sides of the fuselage forward of the cockpit.

Between 1947 and 1948 the Mk III was superseded in front-line units by the F. Mk 4, which was powered by uprated Derwent 5 engines and which went on to equip 22 RAF squadrons. The F. Mk 8, developed from the F.4 had a longer fuselage, extra internal fuel tankage and an ejection seat as standard. The latter safety feature is taken for granted these days but it was not so in the early days of jet fighter aircraft. The Mk 8 had a top speed of 965kph/600mph and from 1950 until 1955 was the RAF's main day interceptor with a staggering 1090 in service to counter the Soviet bomber threat.

Although not used there by the RAF, F.8s of the Royal Australian Air Force became the only British jet aircraft to see action in Korea, though their performance gave the enemy MiG-15s little to worry about. After the type's poor showing against the MiGs in Korea, many air forces applied the Meteor to the ground-attack role, armed with small bombs and air-to-ground rockets. The Meteor's performance was improved during its operational life but by the early 1950s it was outclassed by swept-wing fighters.

RAF F. Mk 8s were replaced by Hunters from 1955 but some were converted for use as target tugs and continued to fly in the RAF until 1977.

TOP: **The F.4 entered RAF service in 1947 and equipped 22 Fighter Command units.** ABOVE: **The Meteor F. Mk III was in RAF service by the end of World War II.** BELOW: **The Meteor was widely exported and equipped the air arms of at least 13 other nations.**

Over 350 Gloster Meteors were exported to at least 13 other nations (NATO air forces included Belgium, the Netherlands and Denmark) and more than 240 were built under licence by Belgium's Avions Fairey. Total UK production of Meteors reached 2920, and a few aircraft dayfighters of the era remained in service for three decades.

Gloster Meteor F. Mk I

First flight: March 5, 1943
Power: Two Rolls-Royce 772kg/1700-lb-thrust W2B/23 Welland turbojets
Armament: Four 20mm/0.78in cannon
Size: Wingspan – 13.11m/43ft
Length – 12.57m/41ft 4in
Height – 3.96m/13ft
Wing area – 34.74m^2/374sq ft
Weights: Empty – 3692kg/8140lb
Maximum take-off – 6268kg/13,800lb
Performance: Maximum speed – 660kph/410mph
Ceiling – 12,190m/40,000ft
Range – 1610km/1000 miles
Climb – 657m/2155ft per minute

Gloster Gladiator

The Gloster Gladiator was the RAF's last biplane fighter and entered service in February 1937, by which time it was already obsolete. Although largely replaced by the start of World War II, the Gladiators of Nos.607 and 615 auxiliary squadrons were deployed to France with the Air Component of the Allied Expeditionary Force in November 1939. The RAF fighter squadrons were converting to Spitfires and Hurricanes when the German attack in the west was launched in May 1940, and the Gladiators proved to be no match for the modern Luftwaffe fighters.

Meanwhile in Norway, No.263 Squadron Gladiators were in action defending British forces and one pilot, Flying Officer Jacobsen, destroyed at least five German aircraft on one remarkable mission. Tragically all of No.263's aircraft and all but two of its pilots were lost when the ship carrying them home following the British withdrawal from Norway was sunk by German battleships.

Even during the Battle of Britain, No.247 Squadron's Gladiators based at Roborough protected Plymouth and its dockyard from German attackers.

In June 1940 a handful of Gladiators were responsible for the defence of Malta and the type was also in action against Italian forces in Egypt. Elsewhere, Gladiators served in the Western Desert until early 1942.

Some Gladiators were fitted with arrester hooks and served with the Fleet Air Arm from December 1938, while fully navalized Sea Gladiators equipped for catapult launches were developed. After withdrawal from front-line duties, Gladiators continued to fly as communications and meteorological aircraft until 1944.

LEFT: **Three RAF Gladiators, literally tied together for the ultimate test of formation flying, practice for the Hendon Air Display.** BELOW: **This Gladiator, preserved in the UK by the Shuttleworth Collection, is shown painted as an aircraft of No.247 Squadron at the time of the Battle of Britain.**

Gloster Gladiator Mk I

First flight: September 12, 1934
Power: Bristol 840hp Mercury IX air-cooled radial piston engine
Armament: Two 7.7mm/0.303in machine-guns in nose, plus two more mounted in wing
Size: Wingspan – 9.83m/32ft 3in
Length – 8.36m/27ft 5in
Height – 3.15m/10ft 4in
Wing area – 30.01m^2/323sq ft
Weights: Empty – 1565kg/3450lb
Maximum take-off – 2155kg/4750lb
Performance: Maximum speed – 407kph/253mph
Ceiling – 10,060m/33,000ft
Range – 547km/340 miles
Climb – 6095m/20,000ft in 9 minutes, 30 seconds

Grumman Biplane fighters

The Grumman company's long association with the US Navy began in March 1931, when the Navy ordered a prototype two-seat biplane fighter, the XFF-1. The all-metal XFF-1 had a top speed of 314kph/195mph and was faster than the Navy's standard fighter of the time, the Boeing F4B-4. The Navy ordered the Grumman biplane and it entered service as the FF-1 from April 1933. Canadian licence-built versions, known as Goblins were supplied to the Royal Canadian Air Force, Nicaragua and Japan. Spanish Republican Forces also acquired 40 of them and the two-seaters were in action against Spanish Nationalist forces between 1936 and 1939, during the Spanish Civil War.

The FF-1 was certainly a winning design and Grumman unsurprisingly began to develop a lighter, single-seat version, which became the F2F-1. The single-seater was lighter than the FF1, had a top speed of 383kph/238mph and entered US Navy service during 1935, replacing the F4B. The F2F-1 remained in front-line service aboard USS *Lexington* until late September 1940, at which point it became an advanced trainer.

The F2F-1 had exhibited some inherent directional instability, which Grumman sought to eradicate in an improved design, the F3F. With a longer fuselage and wings, together with other aero-dynamic refinements, the F3F-1 prototype first flew in March 1935 but crashed two days later, killing the pilot, when the engine and wings detached themselves in a test dive. Wing and engine fittings were strengthened on the second prototype which also crashed, on May 17, after the pilot was unable to recover from a flat spin. Remarkably, this crashed aircraft was rebuilt and was back in the air after just three weeks, fitted with a small ventral fin beneath the tail to aid spin recovery.

ABOVE AND LEFT: **The Grumman F3F was in US Navy service from 1936 until 1941. The family resemblance to the later Wildcat monoplane is clear.**

The F3F-1 entered US Navy service aboard USS *Ranger* and USS *Saratoga* in 1936 and US Marine Corps unit VMF-211 was the last to retire the F3F, in October 1941.

Grumman F2F-1

First flight: October 18, 1933
Power: Pratt & Whitney 650hp R-1535-72 Twin Wasp Junior radial piston engine
Armament: Two 7.62mm/0.3in machine-guns
Size: Wingspan – 8.69m/28ft 6in
Length – 6.53m/21ft 5in
Height – 2.77m/9ft 1in
Wing area – 21.37m^2/230sq ft
Weights: Empty – 1221kg/2691lb
Maximum take-off – 1745kg/3847lb
Performance: Maximum speed – 383kph/238mph
Ceiling – 8380m/27,500ft
Range – 1585km/985 miles
Climb – 939m/3080ft per minute

Grumman F4F Wildcat

If the Wildcat looks like a biplane missing a set of wings there is a good reason – it was originally conceived as a biplane but was redesigned as a monoplane, the F4F, in 1936. Its industrial appearance, due to the entirely riveted fuselage, masked an aircraft with excellent speed and manoeuvrability.

In early 1939 the French Aéronavale placed the first order for the type with Grumman and this was followed in August that year by an order from the US Navy. After France fell, aircraft destined for the Aéronavale were diverted to Britain, where the first machines for Britain's Fleet Air Arm arrived in July 1940. The British named the F4F the "Martlet" and put the type into service almost immediately with No.804 Squadron in the Orkneys. In December 1940 two of these Martlets became the first US-built fighters in British World War II service to destroy a German aircraft. In September 1941 No.802 Squadron became the first FAA unit to go to sea with Martlets, aboard HMS *Audacity*, and on the 20th, two of the aircraft shot down a Focke-Wulf 200 that was shadowing their convoy. Martlets of the Royal Naval Fighter Unit saw action over the Western Desert and shot down an Italian Fiat G.50 on September 28, 1941.

In May 1942 over Madagascar, FAA Martlets saw action against Vichy French aircraft and in August that year, while escorting a convoy to Malta, they tackled Italian bombers over the Mediterranean. By now the Martlet/Wildcat was known as a formidable fighter aircraft. Pilots praised its hard-hitting firepower but knew it was a tricky aircraft to fly and to handle on the ground too.

When the USA entered World War II in December 1941 the F4F, by now known as the Wildcat, was the most widely used fighter on US aircraft carriers and also equipped many

LEFT: **Despite its origins in a biplane design, the F4F went on to be one of the most effective carrier fighters of World War II.** BELOW: **Impressed by the performance of the Wildcat prototype, the US Navy ordered 78 of the type in 1939.**

LEFT: **To survive the harsh environment of carrier operations, naval fighters have to be supremely rugged and the Wildcat was just that.** BELOW: **Royal Navy Wildcats, initially named Martlets, saw widespread action in World War II and destroyed many enemy aircraft.** BOTTOM: **British Fleet Air Arm Wildcats destroyed four Luftwaffe fighters over Norway in March 1945.**

land-based US Marine Corps units. This tough, hard-hitting and highly manoeuvrable aircraft was the US Navy's only carrier-borne fighter until the 1943 arrival of the Hellcat. Wildcats were central to some of the war's most remarkable heroic actions involving US Navy and USMC pilots.

USMC Wildcats operated extensively from land bases, one of which was Henderson Field on Guadalcanal and it was from here that the Americans mounted their first offensive action of the war in the Pacific. One USMC Wildcat pilot, Captain Joe Foss, a flight commander with Marine Fighting Squadron VMF-121, led his flight of eight Wildcats from Guadalcanal to 72 confirmed aerial victories in a matter of sixteen weeks. Foss himself shot down a total of 26 Japanese aircraft, including five in a single day, and was awarded the Congressional Medal of Honor.

Although in a straight fight Wildcats could not cope well with Japanese Zeros, the Grumman fighter's armour plating and self-sealing fuel tanks, together with its pilot's tenacity made it a potent adversary in a dogfight. US Navy Wildcats were phased out in favour of the Grumman Hellcat in late 1943 but Britain's Fleet Air Arm continued to operate the Wildcat to the end of the war. In March 1945 Wildcats (the British abandoned the name Martlet in January 1944) of No.882 Squadron destroyed four Messerschmitt Bf109s over Norway in what was the FAA's last wartime victory over German fighters.

Those Wildcats built by General Motors were designated FM-1 and -2.

Grumman FM-2 Wildcat 

First flight: March 1943 (FM-2)

Power: Wright Cyclone 1350hp R-1820-56 nine-cylinder air-cooled radial engine

Armament: Six 12.7mm/0.5in machine-guns in outer wings, plus two underwing 113kg/250lb bombs or six 12.7cm/5in rockets

Size: Wingspan – 11.58m/38ft
Length – 8.8m/28ft 11in
Height – 3.5m/11ft 5in
Wing area – 24.16m²/260sq ft

Weights: Empty – 2226kg/4900lb
Maximum take-off – 3367kg/7412lb

Performance: Maximum speed – 534kph/332mph
Service ceiling – 10,576m/34,700ft
Range – 1,448km/900 miles
Climb – 610m/2000ft per minute

Grumman F6F Hellcat

The F6F Hellcat has been rightly described as a war-winning fighter. Developed from the F4F Wildcat, designed and produced in record time, the Hellcat's combat début in August 1943 swung the Pacific air power balance firmly in favour of the United States. From then on all the major Pacific air battles were dominated by the F6F. In its first big air battle, in the Kwajalein area on December 4, 1943, 91 Hellcats fought 50 Japanese A6M Zeros and destroyed 28 for the loss of only two. Powered by the Pratt and Whitney R-2800 Double Wasp engine, the robust Hellcat was credited with 75 per cent of all enemy aircraft destroyed by US Navy carrier pilots, with an overall F6F kills-to-losses ratio in excess of 19:1. The Hellcat was America's all-time top "ace-making" aircraft, with no less than 307 pilots credited with the destruction of five or more enemy aircraft while flying the Grumman fighter. US Navy pilot Lt Bill Hardy became an ace on the day of April 6, 1945, when in a single 70-minute sortie he engaged and destroyed five Japanese aircraft.

Effective at any altitude, the Hellcat's unusual features included backwards-retracting landing gear and a distinctive 31.13m²/334sq ft wing, larger than that of any other major single-engined fighter of World War II. The outer sections of the folding wings each contained three 12.7mm/0.5in machine-guns, with 400 rounds each.

Nightfighter versions equipped with radar appeared in early 1944 and ensured that the Hellcats were an ever-present threat to their enemies. The Hellcat omnipresence in Pacific combat zones night or day came to be known as "The Big

TOP: The Hellcat turned the tide in favour of the USA in the Pacific air war during World War II. ABOVE: The XF6F-4, the Hellcat prototype. LEFT: During World War II the F6F was the single-engine fighter with the largest wing area.

Blue Blanket". US Navy ace Lt Alex Vraciu destroyed 19 Japanese aircraft while flying Hellcats, including six in one spectacular eight-minute engagement, and later described the F6F Hellcat as "tough, hard-hitting, dependable – one hell of an airplane".

From April 1943 Britain's Fleet Air Arm received 252 F6F-3s under the Lend Lease programme. Initially renamed the "Gannet" in Royal Navy service, British F6Fs saw a lot of combat in actions off Norway, in the Mediterranean and the Far East, including the final assault on Japan. By late 1945 the Hellcat was virtually completely replaced in Royal Navy service, although a senior Fleet Air Arm officer is known to have had a personal F6F until 1953.

When the last aircraft rolled off the production line in November 1945 it made a total Hellcat production figure of 12,272, of which 11,000 were built in just two years. Swift production of the Hellcat has been attributed to the soundness of the original design, which required few engineering changes while production was underway.

Other nations that operated the Hellcat included France, whose Aéronavale used them in Indo-China, while the Argentine and Uruguayan navies used them until 1961.

Some US Navy Hellcats were converted into drones packed with explosives, and in August 1952 six of these remotely controlled F6F-5Ks were directed on to North Korean targets.

ABOVE: **During the last two years of World War II the Hellcat was credited with 75 per cent of enemy aircraft shot down by US Navy pilots.** BELOW: **In all, the F6F destroyed over 5000 enemy aircraft.** BOTTOM: **US Navy ace Lt Alex Vraciu pictured with his personal Hellcat. This historic aircraft, also pictured below, is preserved in flying condition in the UK.**

Grumman F6F-5 Hellcat

First flight: June 26, 1942
Power: Pratt and Whitney 2000hp R-2800-10W 18-cylinder two-row air-cooled radial piston engine
Armament: Six 12.7mm/0.5in Browning machine-guns, plus provision for bombs up to 907kg/2000lb
Size: Wingspan – 13m/42ft 10in
Length – 10.2m/33ft 7in
Height – 3.96m/13ft
Wing area – 31m^2/334sq ft
Weights: Empty – 4152kg/9153lb
Maximum take-off – 6991kg/15,413lb
Performance: Maximum speed – 621kph/386mph
Ceiling – 11,369m/37,300ft
Range – 1674km/1040 miles on internal fuel
Climb – 1039m/3410ft per minute

Grumman F8F Bearcat

The Grumman Bearcat was the last in the Grumman series of carrier-based fighters that had started back in 1931 with the Grumman FF. It was one of the fastest piston-engined aircraft ever and was built to a specification calling for a small, light fighter aircraft to be powered by the mighty R-2800 Double Wasp engine that had been used in the Hellcat and Tigercat.

The Bearcat was 20 per cent lighter than the Hellcat and had a 30 per cent greater rate of climb than its Grumman stablemate. These factors, together with its excellent manoeuvrability and good low-level performance made it an excellent fighter aircraft in all respects. It is worth noting that in comparative trials the Bearcat's impressive performance allowed it to outmanoeuvre most of the early jet fighters. The first production aircraft (the F8F-1) were delivered in February 1945, a mere six months after the prototype test flight.

In May 1945 US Navy fighter squadron VF-19 became the first unit to equip with the Bearcat but the type arrived too late to see action in World War II. Production nevertheless continued until May 1949, by which time 24 US Navy squadrons were operating Bearcats. The F8F-1B version (of which 100 were built) was armed with four 20mm/0.78in cannon instead of the four 12.7mm/0.5in machine-guns of the F8F-1. Almost 300 examples of the F8F-2 were built with 20mm/0.5in cannon armament as standard. Small numbers of radar-equipped nightfighter and photo-reconnaissance versions were also made.

The Bearcat was phased out of front-line US Navy use by 1952 but around 250 were refurbished and sold as F8F-1Ds to the French Armée de l'Air, who used them in Indo-China. Many of these aircraft were later acquired by the air forces of both North and South Vietnam. The Royal Thai Air Force was also supplied with about 130 Bearcats.

TOP: **The Bearcat was the fastest piston-engined production aircraft ever built and was loved by its pilots.** ABOVE: **Too late for wartime service, the Bearcat remained in front-line US Navy service until the early 1950s.** LEFT: **Due to its high performance, the Bearcat has become a favourite of air racers and warbird collectors.**

Grumman F8F-1B Bearcat

First flight: August 21, 1944
Power: Pratt & Whitney 2100hp R-2800-34W Double Wasp 18-cylinder radial piston engine
Armament: Four 20mm/0.78in cannon, plus provision for two 454kg/1,000lb bombs or four 12.7cm/5in rockets under wings
Size: Wingspan – 10.92m/35ft 10in
Length – 8.61m/28ft 3in Height – 4.2m/13ft 10in
Wing area – 22.67m^2/244sq ft
Weights: Empty – 3206kg/7070lb
Maximum take-off – 5873kg/12,947lb
Performance: Maximum speed – 677kph/421mph
Ceiling – 11,795m/38,700ft
Range – 1778km/1105 miles
Climb – 1395m/4570ft per minute

Hawker Fury

The Fury was loved by its pilots, who praised its light and sensitive controls and excellent rate of climb. This small biplane first flew in March 1931 and on entering Royal Air Force service in May that year, became the first RAF fighter to exceed 322kph/200mph. Displays of aerobatics by RAF Furies were for some years the highlight of the famous Hendon Air Pageants – on some occasions three Furies were literally tied together for a full aerobatic routine, demonstrating how stable and responsive the aircraft could be.

An improved performance version powered by the Kestrel VI engine entered RAF service in early 1937 as the Fury II – this was to serve as a stop gap while the Hurricane was developed. Although the Fury II could fly 10 per cent faster than the Mk I it had 10 per cent less range than the earlier model.

Furies were the main RAF fighters in the mid-1930s and some remained in the RAF front line until 1937, when they were replaced by Gladiators. When World War II broke out in September 1939, around 50 Fury IIs were still in service with training units.

Export versions were supplied to South Africa, Spain, Norway, Persia (Iran), Portugal and Yugoslavia. Three squadrons of South African Furies saw action in East Africa early in World War II, while Yugoslav Furies were pitched against the Luftwaffe during the German invasion of April 1941. The Mk I examples supplied to Persia in 1933 were powered with Pratt and Whitney Hornet or Bristol Mercury radial engines and the RAF came up against some of these Furies during a revolt in 1941.

ABOVE: **This preserved Fury I is a regular at British air shows.** RIGHT: **The Fury was the first Royal Air Force fighter to exceed 322kph/200mph.** BELOW: **Furies were exported to a number of nations including Yugoslavia, who operated the machine pictured.**

Hawker Fury II

First flight: March 25, 1931 (Fury I)
Power: Rolls-Royce 640hp Kestrel VI 12-cylinder V piston engine
Armament: Two synchronized forward-firing 7.7mm/0.303in machine-guns
Size: Wingspan – 9.14m/30ft
Length – 8.15m/26ft 9in
Height – 3.1m/10ft 2in
Wing area – 23.41m^2/252sq ft
Weights: Empty – 1245kg/2743lb
Maximum take-off – 1637kg/3609lb
Performance: Maximum speed – 359kph/223mph
Ceiling – 8990m/29,500ft
Range – 435km/270 miles
Climb – 3050m/10,000ft in 3.8 minutes

Hawker Hurricane

TOP: **Preserved in the UK, this Hurricane is painted as a nightfighter of No.87 Squadron, one of the longest serving RAF Hurricane nightfighter units.**
ABOVE: **The number of airworthy Hurricanes is growing.**

Comparison of the Hurricane and the earlier Hawker Fury's fuselages explains why the embryonic Hurricane was initially known as the Fury Monoplane. The aircraft that only became known as the Hurricane in June 1936 first flew in November 1935, retaining the metal tube construction with fabric covering used by Hawkers since the late 1920s, and not the more modern and complicated stressed-metal fuselage. War clouds were forming in Europe and it was important to get the RAF's first eight-gun monoplane fighter into production and into service as quickly as possible. Stressed-metal covered wings became standard after early Hurricane models appeared with fabric-covered wings.

When the Hurricane entered RAF service, replacing No.111 Squadron's Gloster Gauntlets at Northolt in December 1937, it became the first RAF aircraft able to exceed 482kph/300mph. In February 1938 a 111 Squadron Hurricane flew into the record books by making a nightflight from Edinburgh to RAF Northolt at a very impressive average speed of 656kph/408mph.

Hurricanes outnumbered Spitfires in RAF Fighter Command by about two to one when war broke out and so bore the brunt of early wartime fighter operations. Four squadrons operated in France and on October 30, 1939 a Hurricane of No.1 Squadron destroyed the first German aircraft of World War II, a Dornier Do 17.

It was, however, during the Battle of Britain in 1940 that the Hurricane earned its place in history, accounting for more enemy aircraft than all other defences, ground and air combined. In August of that historic year, Hurricane pilot Flight Lt J.B. Nicholson of No.249 Squadron was awarded Fighter Command's only Victoria Cross for attacking a Luftwaffe Messerschmitt Me110 after his own aircraft had caught fire.

While the Battle of Britain raged, on August 2, 1940, Hurricanes of No.261 Squadron began their defence of Malta against Italian bombers. Hurricanes took on the Italians again, but this time over Britain, in November 1940, during a little-known episode of World War II. Italian bombers made their one and only en masse appearance over the UK and were badly mauled by the Hurricanes of Nos.46, 249 and 257 Squadrons. Seven out of ten Fiat BR.20 bombers were shot down, together with four Fiat CR.42 escort fighters.

The Mk II Hurricane reached RAF squadrons from September 1940 and differed from the Mk I by having a two-stage supercharged Merlin XX engine instead of the

ABOVE: **The world's only surviving Sea Hurricane is preserved in the UK.**

Merlin III. Armament on the Mk II varied between the eight machine-guns of the IIA to the 12 7.7mm/0.303in machine-guns of the IIB. The Mk IIC joined the squadrons in April 1941 and carried four 20mm/0.78in guns.

Nightfighter and navalized versions appeared later and ground-attack variants, some carrying two devastating 40mm/0.79in anti-tank guns (the Mk IID), were widely used in North Africa. Hurricanes operating in Burma became the leading RAF fighter against the Japanese. The last version to enter service was the Mk IV, which equipped the RAF's last Hurricane squadron, No.6, until January 1947. A total of 14,231 Hurricanes were built in Britain and Canada and a handful remain flying today.

In 1941 the Royal Navy began to use Hurricanes fitted with catapult and arrester gear. Known as Sea Hurricanes, they served with the Merchant Ship Fighter Unit and also the Fleet Air Arm from carriers. The former versions were carried on ships on rocket sleds and were launched when a threat appeared. When unable to recover to land or to a carrier the aircraft simply ditched in the sea.

As a fighter, the aircraft was extremely popular with pilots since it was fast, agile and, as celebrated Hurricane pilot Robert Stanford Tuck recalled, "The Hurricane was solid and could obviously stand up to a lot of punishment. It was steady as a rock and an excellent gun platform. Pilot visibility was better than the contemporary Spitfires as the nose sloped more steeply from the cockpit to the spinner and this of course made shooting rather easier".

Hawker Hurricane Mk I

First flight: November 6, 1935

Power: Rolls-Royce 1030hp Merlin III 12-cylinder liquid-cooled engine

Armament: Eight 7.7mm/0.303in Browning machine-guns with 334 rounds per gun

Size: Wingspan – 12.19m/40ft
Length – 9.57m/31ft 5in
Height – 4.m/13ft 1.5in
Wing area – 24m^2/258sq ft

Weights: Empty – 2260kg/4982lb
Loaded – 2924kg/6447lb

Performance: Maximum speed – 511kph/318mph
Ceiling – 10,970m/36,000ft
Range – 740km/460 miles
Climb – 770m/2520ft per minute

TOP: **Turkey was one of the export customers for the Hurricane.** MIDDLE: **Though eclipsed by the Spitfire, the Hurricane was central to the British victory in the Battle of Britain.** BOTTOM: **A pre-war examination of a No.1 Squadron RAF aircraft.**

Hawker Tempest

The Tempest was developed from the Typhoon and differed from its predecessor mainly by its lengthened fuselage and a new thin-section laminar flow wing intended to improve on the Typhoon's disappointing climb and altitude performance. Five versions were planned to test various engine installations but only three ever saw service – the Mks II, V and VI. On the Mk II Tempest the radiator was moved from beneath the engine to the wing leading edges and fuel tankage moved from the wing to the longer fuselage. The first Tempest to fly, the Mk V, was a modified Typhoon which took to the air in September 1942.

The V was powered by a Napier Sabre II engine, while the Mk VI had the 2340hp Sabre V. Only the Tempest Mk V, retaining the Typhoon's distinctive chin radiator, saw wartime service, the first RAF Tempest wing being formed in April 1944. After initial train-busting and ground-attack duties, the Tempest V was used to tackle the V-1 flying bombs and excelled in the role. The Tempest V was the fastest fighter to be responsible for British air defence and destroyed 638 V-1s between June 13 and September 5, 1944.

Later, as part of the 2nd Tactical Air Force, Tempest Vs destroyed 20 Messerschmitt Me262s in air combat. Post-war, a number of Tempest Vs continued to serve as target tugs, and the Tempest VI was the RAF's standard Middle East fighter until the Vampire replaced them in 1949.

The Tempest II looked very different from the earlier Typhoon and was powered by a 2520hp Centaurus engine. It was designed for operations against the Japanese but the war ended before they could be deployed as part of the planned Tiger Force.

The Mk II first entered RAF service in November 1945 and the majority served overseas. Three Tempest II squadrons were based in Germany in 1946–8 and during the Berlin Airlift in 1948–9 Tempests of No.33 Squadron were based at Berlin's RAF Gatow to demonstrate the RAF's fighter potential in the area. No.33 later operated their Tempest IIs in the Far East and some saw action against Malayan terrorists in 1950–1.

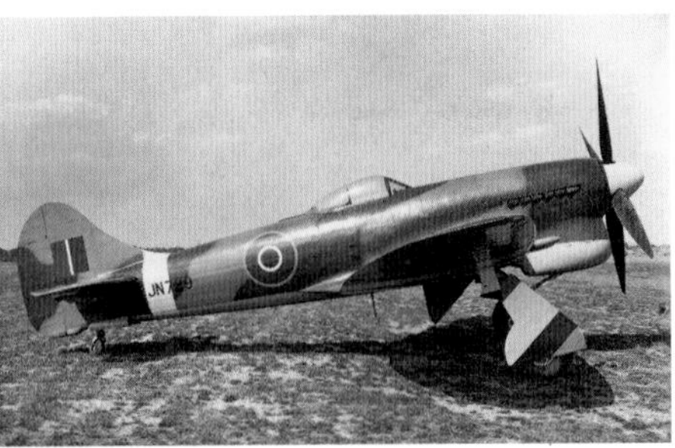

ABOVE: **The Tempest's Typhoon origins are clear in this photograph of a Mk V – note the bubble canopy introduced in later Typhoons for improved pilot view.** BELOW: **Post-war, this Tempest V was used for target towing duties.**

Hawker Tempest V

First flight: September 1942
Power: Napier 2180-hp Sabre II 24-cylinder piston engine
Armament: Four 20mm/0.78in cannon in wings and provision for rocket-projectiles or 908kg/2000lb of bombs beneath wings
Size: Wingspan – 12.5m/41ft
Length – 10.26m/33ft 8in
Height – 4.9m/16ft 1in
Wing area – 28.06m^2/302sq ft
Weights: Empty – 4082kg/9000lb
Maximum take-off – 6142kg/13,500lb
Performance: Maximum speed – 686kph/427mph
Ceiling – 11,125m/36,500ft
Range – 1191km/740 miles
Climb – 4575m/15,000ft in 5 minutes

Hawker Typhoon

The Typhoon was plagued with engine problems and structural weaknesses in its early days and failed to perform adequately for its intended role as a wartime interceptor. Nevertheless it went on to become an extremely effective fighter-bomber, accompanying the Allied advance through France and Holland in the later stages of World War II in 1944.

The Typhoon was born of a British Air Ministry specification for an interceptor designed to make the most of the new Rolls-Royce and Napier 24-cylinder 2000hp engines then under development. The Typhoon was paired with the Napier Sabre engine and flew for the first time in February 1940. Continued development and production problems delayed the Typhoon's delivery to the RAF until August 1941, when it became the RAF's first 643kph/400mph fighter. The price to pay for the high speed was a low rate of climb and lacklustre performance at altitude, all due to the unreliable Sabre engine, which simply entered service before it was ready. A hazard unrelated to engine problems for early Typhoon pilots was a structural weakness in the tail, which cost the lives of a number of pilots – this problem was later rectified.

ABOVE: **A Typhoon IB of No.175 Squadron RAF is checked and armed for another D-Day period mission.**

BELOW LEFT: **This unusual trials Typhoon IB, built by Gloster Aircraft, is shown with a four-blade propeller.**

BELOW RIGHT: **A No.183 Squadron Typhoon IB – the "Tiffie" was the only RAF fighter with the speed to stop Fw190 hit-and-run raids on Britain.**

The whole Typhoon fleet was almost withdrawn from service, such was the effect of the combined problems, but these were fixed and a use was found for the Typhoon's high low-level speed. German Focke-Wulf 190s had been carrying out hit-and-run raids along Britain's south coast – the Typhoon with its top speed of 664kph/412mph was the only RAF fighter that could catch them and destroyed four within days of being deployed.

From 1943, "Tiffies" went on the offensive, attacking targets in France and the Low Countries. When late in 1943 the Typhoons began carrying rocket projectiles, they proved to be truly devastating aircraft. The relentless day and night attacks by RAF Typhoon squadrons on German communications targets greatly aided the D-Day operations. The aircraft that was once almost scrapped from RAF service ultimately equipped no fewer than 26 squadrons of the 2nd Tactical Air Force.

Hawker Typhoon IB

First flight: May 27, 1941 (Production IA)
Power: Napier 2180hp Sabre IIA 24-cylinder sleeve-valve liquid-cooled piston engine
Armament: Four 20mm/0.78in cannon in outer wings and racks for eight rockets or two 227kg/500lb bombs
Size: Wingspan – 12.67m/41ft 7in
Length – 9.73m/31ft 11in
Height – 4.67m/15ft 4in
Wing area – 25.92m^2/279sq ft
Weights: Empty – 3992kg/8800lb
Maximum take-off – 6010kg/13,250lb
Performance: Maximum speed – 664kph/412mph
Ceiling – 10,730m/35,200ft
Range – 821km/510 miles (with bombs)
Climb – 914m/3000ft per minute

Heinkel He219

Heinkel's excellent nightfighter began as project P.1060 in 1940 as a high-speed multi-role aircraft. There was little interest in the design until late 1941, when RAF Bomber Command's raids began to have a strategic impact on the German war machine. Ernst Heinkel was then asked to produce his design as a nightfighter and so it first flew in November 1942. Among the design innovations were a tricycle undercarriage (the first operational Luftwaffe aircraft to have one) and ejection seats (the first anywhere in an operational aircraft) that accommodated the pilot and navigator in tandem but back to back.

The second prototype was evaluated in mock combat against other Luftwaffe types and was so successful that a production order was placed immediately.

The He219 Uhu (eagle-owl), equipped with radar that could find enemy bombers in the dark and a formidable armament with which to destroy them, was clearly a fearsome night-fighter and the Luftwaffe were keen to get it into service. So keen in fact that even the early prototypes were sent to form a trials unit at Venlo in Holland in April 1943. On the night of June 11, Major Werner Streib shot down five RAF Lancaster bombers in one sortie, thus proving the military value of dedicated nightfighter aircraft. During the first six night missions an incredible 20 RAF bombers were claimed as destroyed, among them six Mosquitoes. Despite this success, the He219 was never produced in adequate numbers, mainly because a bewildering profusion of sub-types appeared, with different armament and "black box" installations, to prove the aircraft's worth to sceptical officials. From November 1944 virtually the only aircraft being produced were jets and so the He219 only ever totally equipped one unit, 1/NJG 1, based at Venlo. Individual aircraft were attached to other units but the type was never used strategically. The Uhu was another fine German design that did not reach its potential due to the short-sightedness or sheer incompetence of the decision-makers within the Luftwaffe and government.

TOP: **The He219 was an extremely effective nightfighter that wreaked havoc among RAF bombing raids.** ABOVE: **This He219A-7, an aircraft operated by 3/NJG (Nachtjagdgeschwader – nightfighter wing) 3, was evaluated after the war by the RAF.** LEFT: **One of many sub-types, the prototype A-5/R1.**

Heinkel He219A-7/R2 Uhu

First flight: November 15, 1942
Power: Two Daimler-Benz 1800hp DB603E 12-cylinder engines
Armament: Four 20mm/0.78in cannon – two in underbelly "tray" and two in wing roots. Two 30mm/1.18in cannon, mounted to fire obliquely forward from rear of cockpit
Size: Wingspan – 18.5m/60ft 8.3in
Length – 16.34m/53ft 7.25in
Height – 4.1m/13ft 5.4in
Wing area – 44.5m²/478.99sq ft
Weights: Empty – 8345kg/18,398lb
Maximum take-off – 15,100kg/33,289lb
Performance: Maximum speed – 460kph/286mph
Ceiling – 9800m/32,150ft
Range – 1850km/1150 miles
Climb – 552m/1810ft per minute

LEFT: **The I.A.R. 80 was a lesser-known fighter type that served for some years after World War II.**

I.A.R. 80

First flight: April 1939
Power: I.A.R. 1025hp K14-1000A radial piston engine
Armament: Four 7.92mm/0.31in machine-guns in wings
Size: Wingspan – 10.5m/34ft 5.25in
Length – 8.9m/29ft 2.5in Height – 3.6m/11ft 9.75in
Wing area – 15.97m²/171.9sq ft
Weights: Empty – 1780kg/3924lb
Maximum take-off – 2550kg/5622lb
Performance: Maximum speed – 550kph/342mph
Ceiling – 10,500m/34,450ft
Range – 940km/584 miles
Climb – 4500m/14,760ft in 5 minutes, 40 seconds

I.A.R. 80

The I.A.R. 80 was derived from the Polish-designed P.Z.L. P-24 fighter and was designed to replace the P-24. Development work was exclusively Romanian and began in 1938. The resulting fighter that first flew in April 1939 was tough and offered a drastically improved performance over the P-24. The front and rear of the two aircraft were almost identical. The significant difference was in the wholly new centre section. The bubble-type canopy was very advanced for the time and offered the pilot excellent visibility. Production was carried out on German authority and later models carried the German Mauser cannon. Strangely the type had a skid instead of a tailwheel.

About 250 were built in a number of versions and most served on the Eastern Front from May 1942. From 1943 all were based in Romania defending the country from US bomber attacks.

About half of all produced survived the war and served with the Romanian Air Force, this time under Soviet control, until they were replaced by Soviet fighters from 1949. A number were converted into two-seat dual control trainers and were in service until 1952.

LEFT: **A Ju 88 nightfighter bristling with radar aerials. The Ju 88 was the most versatile combat aircraft in the wartime Luftwaffe inventory.**

Junkers Ju 88G

First flight: December 21, 1936 (Ju 88 prototype)
Power: Two BMW 1700hp 801D-2 14-cylinder radials
Armament: Two 30mm/1.18in and up to six 20mm/0.78in cannon
Size: Wingspan – 20m/65ft 7in
Length – 14.54m/47ft 8in
Height – 4.85m/15ft 11in
Wing area – 54.5m/586.6sq ft
Weights: Empty – 9081kg/20,020lb
Maximum take-off – 14,690kg/32,385lb
Performance: Maximum speed – 573kph/356mph
Ceiling – 8840m/29,000ft
Range – 4 hours endurance
Climb – 504.78m/1655ft per minute

Junkers Ju 88

The Ju 88 is widely described as the "German Mosquito" because, like the de Havilland Mosquito, the Ju 88 was an extremely versatile design. It was first designed as a high-speed bomber but was then developed for dive-bomber, torpedo-bomber, close support, reconnaissance, heavy fighter and nightfighter roles. The Ju 88's speed, almost as good as fighters of the time, led to the C-series of heavy fighters and the first, the Ju 88C-0, made its maiden flight in July 1939. Large numbers of C-series fighters were eventually built, powered by Jumo 211 or BMW 801 engines, with solid noses housing a battery of cannon and machine-guns.

The Ju 88G was the definitive radar-equipped three-seat nightfighter, with typical armament of two 30mm/1.18in plus four to six 20mm/0.78in cannon all firing diagonally forward and upwards to destroy bombers with a short but deadly burst of fire from below.

Ju 88 nightfighters were one of the most effective German defences against enemy bombers.

Kawanishi N1K1-/K2-J

Land-based aircraft have often been turned into floatplanes, but in the case of the Kawanishi N1K1-J Shiden (violet lightning), it was uniquely a landplane derived from a floatplane fighter. Codenamed "George" by the Allies, it entered service during the last year of World War II, appearing throughout the Pacific from May 1944. In spite of production problems and shortages of parts caused by B-29 raids on the Japanese homeland, over 1400 were built and were formidable foes. Manoeuvrability was dramatically enhanced by unique automatic combat flaps that increased lift during extreme combat manoeuvres. The George proved to be one of the best all-round fighters in the Pacific theatre but lacked the high-altitude performance needed to counter the devastating B-29 raids.

Early versions had poor visibility due to the mid-mounted wing and inadequate landing gear and so the N1K2-J version known as the Shiden-Kai was produced. The main difference was the moving of the wing from mid to low position, which reduced the need for troublesome long landing gear. The prototype of this variant first flew in December 1943, and was soon adopted as the standard Japanese land-based fighter and fighter-bomber. The N1K2-J could be built in half the time of the earlier version and became a truly outstanding fighter aircraft, which could hold its own against the best of Allied fighters.

LEFT: **The N1K1 Kyofu (mighty wind) floatplane fighter from which the "George" derived.**
BELOW: **The Shiden-Kai was an excellent fighter, but a number were used as kamikaze aircraft.**

Kawanishi N1K2-J

First flight: December 31, 1943
Power: Nakajima 1990hp NK9H Homare 21 radial piston engine
Armament: Four 20mm/0.78in cannon in wings plus two 250kg/551lb bombs under wings
Size: Wing span – 12m/39ft 4.5in
Length – 9.35m/30ft 8in
Height – 3.96m/13ft
Wing area – 23.5m^2/252.96sq ft
Weights: Empty – 2657kg/5858lb
Maximum take-off – 4860kg/10,714lb
Performance: Maximum speed – 595kph/370mph
Ceiling – 10,760m/35,300ft
Range – 2335km/1451 miles with drop tanks
Climb – 1000m/3300ft per minute

Kawasaki Ki-45 Toryu

In 1937, the Imperial Japanese Army issued a requirement for its first long-range twin-engine fighter and Kawasaki's proposal was the Ki-45, which first flew in January 1939. Continued problems with engines delayed production until September 1941, when the aircraft was designated Ki-45 Kai Toryu – kai was short for kaizo (modified) and Toryu means "dragon slayer". The two-seat Toryu finally entered service in August the following year and first saw combat in October 1942. The fast and manoeuvrable Ki-45, codenamed "Nick" by the Allies, achieved a number of victories over USAAF B-24s – the aircraft was then modified for nightfighter duties when the American bombers began to operate at night. It proved so successful as a night-fighter that a specially developed nightfighter version (Kai-C) was produced, fitted with cannon that fired obliquely upward for attacks from below. On the night of June 15, 1944 alone, seven B-29s were claimed by Ki-45s.

In May 1944 four Ki-45s carried out the first kamikaze (divine wind) suicide attacks against Allied ships. More conventional anti-shipping and ground attack variants were also produced. Around 1700 Ki-45s were built.

TOP: **The Imperial Japanese Army's first long-range twin-engine fighter.** ABOVE: **The type was one of the most successful Japanese nightfighters.** LEFT: **Note the two obliquely firing cannon between the cockpits.**

Kawasaki Ki-45 Kai-C Toryu

First flight: January 1939
Power: Two Mitsubishi 1080hp Ha-102 14-cylinder two-row radial piston engines
Armament: Two 12.7mm/0.5in machine-guns, installed at 30 degrees between cockpits, two 12.7mm/0.5in machine-guns and one 20mm/0.78in or 37mm/1.46in cannon in nose, plus one rear-firing 7.92mm/0.31in machine-gun
Size: Wingspan – 15.05m/49ft 4.5in
Length – 11m/36ft 1in Height – 3.7m/12ft 1.5in
Wing area – 32m²/344.46sq ft
Weights: Empty – 4000kg/8820lb
Maximum take-off – 5500kg/12,125lb
Performance: Maximum speed – 545kph/339mph
Ceiling – 10,000m/32,810ft
Range – 2000km/1243 miles
Climb – 700m/2300ft per minute

Kawasaki Ki-61 Hien

The Kawasaki Ki-61 Hien (swallow) fighter was a major departure in Japanese fighter aircraft design in World War II. While other Japanese fighters were designed with air-cooled radials, the Ki-61 used a licence-built Daimler-Benz 601A liquid-cooled in-line engine and was designed for speed. The Ki-61 was so radically different from other Japanese fighters that when the type was first encountered in combat in June 1943, the Allies thought it was a licence-built German or Italian fighter, the latter theory earning Hien the Allied codename of "Tony".

The very different nature of the design makes sense, given that from 1923 to 1933 Kawasaki Aircraft Engineering Company's head designer was Dr Richard Vogt, a German who returned to his homeland in 1933 for a similar role at Blohm und Voss during World War II. Kawasaki continued to be influenced by Vogt's design work long after he left.

The Hien was in constant use from its entry into service in August 1942 until the end of the war, but found itself increasingly outclassed. The Ki-100 was a "Tony" with a radial engine and proved to be an extremely good fighter.

ABOVE: **At one time the Ki-61 was thought to be a version of the Messerschmitt Bf109.** BELOW: **This captured "Tony" was taken for evaluation to the US Naval Air Station Patuxent River.** BOTTOM: **The Ki-61 was Japan's only in-line engined fighter in service during World War II.**

Kawasaki Ki-61-Ic Hien

First flight: December 1941

Power: Kawasaki 1175hp Ha-40 V12 liquid-cooled piston engine

Armament: Two 12.7mm/0.5in machine-guns on top of engine, plus two wing-mounted 20mm/0.78in cannon

Size: Wingspan – 12m/39ft 4.5in
Length – 8.95m/29ft 4.25in
Height – 3.7m/12ft 1.75in
Wing area – 20m^2/215.29sq ft

Weights: Empty – 2630kg/5798lb
Maximum take-off – 3470kg/7650lb

Performance: Maximum speed – 560kph/348mph
Ceiling – 10,000m/32,810ft
Range – 1900km/1181 miles
Climb – 675m/2200ft per minute

Lavochkin LaGG-3 and La-5

The stopgap Lavochkin LaGG-3, built almost entirely of wood, was probably the greatest under-achiever of the early World War II fighters and was easily outclassed by the Messerschmitt Bf109 and Focke-Wulf 190. Even the few Italian Macchi 202s that served on the Russian Front outclassed the Lavochkins.

In 1941 development began on upgrading the powerplant of the LaGG-3's sound airframe by a shift from in-line V-12 engines to an M-82 14-cylinder, twin-row radial engine. Various changes were made to improve both performance and range, and the ever-present need for the use of strategically non-important materials was observed. The resulting aircraft, the La-5, was the first in a series of excellent radial-engined thoroughbred fighters. The Lavochkin La-5FN, again constructed almost wholly of wood, became one of the best Soviet fighters of World War II. The Shvestov M-82 engine had a two-stage supercharger and gave the La-5FN a maximum speed of 648km/403mph. The fighter was responsive, could outperform any other Soviet fighter and, more importantly, almost all of its opponents. Armed with two 20mm/0.9in cannon, the La-5FN could deliver a small but deadly punch. After service with the Russians in World War II, the La-5FN went on to serve for a decade or so with various Soviet bloc countries, until being replaced by jets.

Further improved performance for the La-5 was, however, achieved by weight-saving and aerodynamic fine-tuning undertaken in late 1943, resulting in the high-altitude interceptor designated La-7. Over 5500 of these improved Lavochkins were built by 1946 and saw extensive wartime use.

TOP: **The LaGG-3's all-wooden construction was, among fighters, unique for its time.** ABOVE: **An La-5 of the 1st Czech Fighter Regiment, pictured in the Ukraine.** LEFT: **The higher flying La-7 was built in great quantities.**

Lavochkin La-5FN

First flight: January 1942
Power: Shvetsov 1330hp M-82A 14-cylinder two-row radial engine
Armament: Two 23mm/0.9in cannon, plus underwing bombs
Size: Wingspan – 9.8m/32ft 2in
Length – 8.46m/27ft 10.75in
Height – 2.84m/9ft 3in
Wing area – 17.5m²/188.37sq ft
Weights: Empty – 2800kg/6173lb
Maximum take-off – 3360kg/7407lb
Performance: Maximum speed – 648kph/403mph
Ceiling – 9500m/31,170ft
Range – 765km/475 miles
Climb – 5000m/16,405ft in 4 minutes, 42 seconds

Lockheed P-38 Lightning

The P-38 Lightning's radical twin-boom, twin-engine configuration was Lockheed's answer to an exacting US Army Air Corps specification, in February 1937, for a high-performance long-range interceptor capable of flying at high altitude and high speed for at least an hour.

The P-38 was Lockheed's first purely military type and the prototype, the XP-38, first flew in January 1939. It made headlines almost immediately when it set a new record of 7 hours, 2 minutes for a transcontinental flight across America, even though at 6713kg/14,800lb it weighed more than most American light bombers of the time. From the outset the P-38 was designed as a hard-hitting fighter, being armed with a cannon and four machine-guns in the nose.

In spite of some official misgivings about its high cost and the sheer number of innovations incorporated into the P-38, it entered USAAC service in August 1941. The British had expressed interest in the P-38 but the American ban on the export of superchargers to Europe left the aircraft underpowered in the view of British test pilots. Aircraft were already on the production line earmarked for the RAF but these were diverted for US use when British interest waned. The British apparently named the P-38 "Lightning" and the name was already in widespread use.

Most early models were used for evaluation in the USA but during 1942–3 12 squadrons were equipped with P-38Es in the South West Pacific and the Aleutians. Even before that, an Iceland-based P-38E had claimed the first USAAF destruction of an enemy aircraft in World War II on December 7, 1941. A Focke-Wulf Condor was destroyed only hours after America's declaration of war.

TOP: The radical twin-boom P-38 was a hard-hitting fighter capable of going deep into enemy territory. ABOVE: Regular P-38 combat missions were first flown from Africa.

By this time the P-38's outstanding performance had unsurprisingly led to a reconnaissance version, known as the F-4, and later the F-5, armed only with cameras.

The P-38 came to be deployed extensively in the Pacific, Mediterranean and Europe where the P-38's speed, performance and firepower soon prompted the nickname "fork-tailed devil" from the Germans.

The J model of the P-38 had improved airscrews for better speed and climb at altitude and carried more fuel than earlier versions. With drop tanks, the P-38J had a range of around 3700km/2300 miles, enabling it to fly deep into the heart of enemy territory, engage in ten minutes of air combat and then make it back to the UK. Top speed of the P-38J was 666kph/414mph but in combat dives, pilots frequently exceeded 885kph/550mph. At that speed the aircraft's handling proved difficult and hydraulically assisted control systems were introduced, becoming one of the first examples of power-assisted controls in a combat aircraft.

Some P-38Js were modified to two-seaters equipped with a Norden bombsight, carried a bombardier and led formations of Lightning fighter-bombers on high-altitude precision bombing missions. As the P-47 and P-51 fighters appeared in huge numbers, the Lightnings in Europe were used more and more in the ground-attack and tactical bombing role.

However in the Pacific theatre, the Lightning equipped 27 USAAF squadrons and was credited with the destruction of more enemy aircraft than any other type. As a long-range fighter it was peerless. The top US ace of World War II, Major Richard Bong, earned all his 40 kills flying Lightnings in the Pacific. The most celebrated P-38 mission was probably the interception and destruction of the aircraft carrying Japan's Admiral Yamamoto. The P-38s responsible for this daring mission were from 339th Fighter Squadron on Guadalcanal, operating some 805km/500 miles from their base, using drop tanks to get the extra range. The 347th Fighter Group pilot credited with this remarkable feat was Lt Thomas G. Lanphier, who went on to become a Lockheed test pilot.

ABOVE: **In the Pacific theatre the P-38 equipped 27 USAAF squadrons. The P-38 destroyed more enemy aircraft than any other Allied fighter.**

RIGHT: **The five-gun nose armament is clear on this aircraft painted as the aircraft of P-38 ace Jack Ilfrey.** BELOW: **The P-38's long range made it ideal for the war in the Pacific, where combats were fought over great distances.**

Lockheed P-38J Lightning

First flight: January 27, 1939

Power: Two Allison 1425hp V-1710-89 in-line piston engines

Armament: One 20mm/0.78in cannon, plus four 12.7mm/0.5in machine-guns in nose, up to 908kg/2000lb of bombs and ten 12.7cm/5in rocket projectiles

Size: Wingspan – 15.85m/52ft
Length – 11.52m/37ft 10in
Height – 2.99m/9ft 10in
Wing area – 30.42m²/327.5sq ft

Weights: Empty – 5707kg/12,580lb
Maximum take-off – 9798kg/21,600lb

Performance: Maximum speed – 666kph/414mph
Ceiling – 13,411m/44,000ft
Range – 3636km/2260 miles
Climb – 1524m/5000ft in 2 minutes

Messerschmitt Bf109

The Messerschmitt Bf109, the most famous German fighter of the World War II era, remained in production over a decade after the regime that spawned it was crushed. It first flew in September 1935, powered by a Rolls-Royce Kestrel engine and incorporating features of the Messerschmitt Bf108 four-seat touring aircraft. Messerschmitt 109Bs were first delivered to the Luftwaffe in 1937, to its "top guns" in Jagdgeschwader 132 "Richthofen". Later that year the 109 earned its spurs when it made its combat début with Germany's Condor Legion in the Spanish Civil War. This was invaluable, not only as combat experience for Germany's fighter pilots but also to help with developing and improving what was clearly already an exceptional fighter aircraft.

In November 1937 the 109 flew into the record books by setting a new world landplane speed record of 610.55kph/379.38mph. B, C and D versions all saw service but the type really came into its own with the definitive E model that appeared in late 1938 and was widely deployed at the outbreak of World War II, when the Luftwaffe had around 1000 of these fast and manoeuvrable fighters in service.

TOP AND ABOVE: **Two photographs of the very rare Messerschmitt Bf109G owned by the Royal Air Force Museum and returned to flying condition in the 1990s. Unfortunately the aircraft was damaged in a crash landing and will not fly again.**

The 109E was in action throughout the Blitzkrieg and in this first year of the war outclassed all the fighters it encountered, except the Spitfire. Like the famous Supermarine aircraft, the Messerschmitt 109 will be forever associated with the air fighting that took place in the Battle of Britain in 1940. In fact the 109's first action against the RAF had been on December 18, 1939, when 109Es attacked unescorted Vickers Wellington bombers on a daylight bombing mission over Wilhelmshaven.

Numerous versions of the 109E were in use during the Battle of Britain, including the E-4/B fighter-bomber. The 109 had two main advantages over the British Spitfires and Hurricanes. One was that the cannon armament carried by the Messerschmitt had a longer range and was more damaging

than the rifle-calibre guns of the British fighters. The other fundamental advantage enjoyed by the 109 was the fuel-injection system of its Daimler-Benz engine, which continued to supply fuel no matter how violent the aircraft's manoeuvres. The Merlin engines of the RAF fighters, at the time equipped with carburettors, could, in contrast, be momentarily starved of fuel and cut out if the aircraft was pushed into a steep dive, thus generating negative gravity. RAF pilots soon developed the technique of rolling their aircraft over at the critical time and diving upside down so as not to lose the upper hand in what was often a kill or be killed air combat situation.

By early 1941 the "Emil", as the E model was widely known, had appeared in the Mediterranean theatre and tropicalized versions were serving in North Africa. After the success of the E model the 109F was developed and is considered by many to be the best version of all because of its high speed and excellent all-round performance. While in the West the 109F was able to outclass the Spitfire V, on the Eastern Front it spearheaded the attack on the USSR. At this stage in the 109 story it is worth making the point that throughout its life the 109 was fitted with a bewildering array of armament options, the F-model more than most.

After 1942 the G ("Gustav") became the standard model in Luftwaffe use and was numerically the most important version. Although well-armed, the Gustav needed great attention from the pilot and was particularly difficult to land satisfactorily. It served on all fronts in roles that included fighter-bomber, ground-attack and interceptor.

Post-war, the 109 remained in production, thanks to the Czech firm Avia who had an intact Bf109 factory. In 1948, Israel bought some 109s and used them in combat, while the Spanish Air Force also operated Spanish-built versions. In 1953, Spanish manufacturers began fitting Merlin engines to produce the Buchón (pigeon) and the last new-build 109 was test-flown in 1956. Total production exceeded 35,000.

TOP LEFT: **Incredibly, Spanish-built 109s (Buchons), powered by Rolls-Royce Merlins, were still being built in the mid-1950s.** TOP RIGHT: **The Bf109 was the principal fighter of the wartime Luftwaffe and destroyed more aircraft in combat than any other German fighter.** ABOVE: **Ten prototype Bf109s were built to prove the design in 1935–6 and the type entered Luftwaffe service in 1937.** BELOW: **One of the most widely produced fighter aircraft in history, the Bf109.**

Messerschmitt Bf109E-7

First flight: September 1935

Power: One Daimler-Benz 1200hp DB 601N liquid-cooled inverted-V 12-cylinder piston engine

Armament: One hub-firing 20mm/0.78in cannon and four 7.9mm/0.31in machine-guns, two in engine cowling and two in wings

Size: Wingspan 9.86m/32ft 4.5in
Length – 8.74m/28ft 8in Height – 3.4m/11ft 2in
Wing area – 16.16m^2/174sq ft

Weights: Empty – 2014kg/4440lb
Maximum take-off – 2767kg/6100lb

Performance: Maximum speed – 578kph/358mph
Ceiling – 11,125m/36,500ft
Range – 1094km/680 miles
Climb – 1006m/3300ft per minute

Messerschmitt Bf110

The Bf110 was designed to a Luftwaffe specification for a heavy fighter that could also be used as a high-speed bomber and the prototype flew in 1936. It was intended to escort bombers deep into enemy territory and what it may have lacked in manoeuvrability,

it made up for with firepower. The 110 first saw action during the invasion of Poland and made its mark as a bomber-destroyer in December 1939, when it was used against a force of 22 RAF Wellington bombers and shot down nine. With its capability proven, production was stepped up and over 100 were produced each month during 1940. It was, however, during 1940 that the Bf110 began to suffer heavy losses to more modern fighters such as the Spitfire and Hurricane. Although largely withdrawn as a day fighter, some persisted in this role against better aircraft until 1944, sustaining increasingly heavy losses. After a period of use on bombing and reconnaissance, the type found its niche during the winter of 1940–1 as a nightfighter defending Hitler's Reich.

At first the three-man crews had no special equipment for night operations and relied on their eyes alone to find enemy aircraft in the dark. Ground-controlled interception began from mid-1941, and the 110 began to take its toll of RAF bombers and was soon an aircraft to be feared. Airborne radar was used experimentally during 1941, effective up to a maximum distance of 3.5km/2.2 miles and capable of bringing the 110 to within 200m/655ft of a target. Front-line units received the radar from July 1942. By this time the standard version of the nightfighter was the Bf110F-4, with the usual armament of four 7.92mm/0.31in machine-guns and two 20mm/0.78in cannon. The usual means of attack was from below, the target bomber being raked across the belly and wing fuel tanks with high explosive and incendiary ammunition as the Bf110 pilot pulled the aircraft up. In 1943 the armament was supplemented by upward-firing cannon, which meant the Bf110 only had to formate below the target aircraft to achieve a first-rate firing position.

These nightfighters continued to defend Germany right through to the end of the war and one pilot, Major Heinz-Wolfgang Schnaufer, claimed no less than 121 night kills while flying the Bf110.

Messerschmitt Bf110G/R3 nightfighter

First flight: May 12, 1936
Power: Two Daimler-Benz 1474hp DB 601B-1 inverted V-12 piston engines
Armament: Two 30mm/1.18in cannon and two 20mm/0.78in cannon in nose, plus two 7.92mm/0.31in machine-guns mounted in rear cockpit
Size: Wingspan – 16.25m/53ft 3.75in
Length – 13.05m/42ft 9.75in
Height – 4.18m/13ft 8.5in
Wing area – 38.4m^2/413.35sq ft
Weights: Empty – 5090kg/11,222lb
Maximum take-off – 9890kg/21,804lb
Performance: Maximum speed – 550kph/342mph
Ceiling – 8000m/26,245ft
Range – 2100km/1305 miles with drop tanks
Climb – 661m/2170ft per minute

LEFT: **This Bf110 nightfighter is preserved by the RAF Museum in Britain.** BELOW: **The Bf110 was a key aircraft in the Blitzkrieg.**

Messerschmitt Me410

On the basis of the Bf110's early successes, its manufacturers were asked to design a successor – this became the Me210. The aircraft was certainly a handful on its test flight and was essentially unstable, being prone to stalling and spinning. In spite of this it was ordered into production and 200 were built before it was abandoned in favour of a new production run of Bf110s.

The Me210 design was salvaged with a redesigned, longer, rear fuselage and automatic leading edge slats to counter the stall tendency. Fitted with more powerful engines than the original Me210, the new two-seat heavy fighter aircraft was designated Me410 and called Hornisse (Hornet).

The first Me410As reached front-line Luftwaffe units in January 1943, replacing Dornier Do 217s and Junkers Ju 88s. They were at first used as nightfighter-bombers over Britain and then as bomber-destroyers in the Mediterranean theatre. From Spring 1944 the Hornisse began to replace the Bf110 in bomber-destroyer (Zerstörer) units in defence of the Reich and also served as a nightfighter on the Eastern Front.

The Me410A-1/U4 bomber-destroyer carried a 50mm/2in gun beneath the fuselage that weighed 900kg/1984lb and had a recoil effect of seven tons. Carrying 21 rounds, the effect of the weapon on enemy bombers would have been devastating while the effect on Me410 crews was at best startling and at worst terrifying.

The Me410 was no more effective than the Bf110 it was designed to replace but over 1100 were built before production ceased in September 1944.

TOP: **This excellent preserved example of an Me410 is part of the Royal Air Force Museum collection in Britain.** ABOVE: **The Hornisse was almost identical to the earlier Me210.** LEFT: **This Me410A-3 was captured in Italy and evaluated by the RAF while bearing the serial TF209.**

Messerschmitt Me410A-1/U2 Hornisse

First flight: Late 1942
Power: Two Daimler-Benz 1850hp 603A inverted V-12 in-line piston engines
Armament: Four 20mm/0.78in cannon and two 7.93mm/0.31in machine-guns, plus two 13mm/0.51in remotely controlled rear-firing barbettes
Size: Wingspan – 16.35m/53ft7.75in
Length – 12.48m/40ft 11.5in
Height – 4.28m/14ft 0.5in
Wing area – 36.2m²/389.67sq ft
Weights: Empty – 7518kg/16,574lb
Maximum take-off – 9650kg/21,276lb
Performance: Maximum speed – 625kph/388mph
Ceiling – 10,000m/32,180ft
Range – 1690km/1050 miles
Climb – 6700m/22,000ft in 10 minutes, 42 seconds

Messerschmitt Me163

When the German Komet first attacked USAAF bomber formations in July 1944 it struck fear into the Allies. This extremely high-performance rocket-powered fighter flew almost twice as fast as any Allied fighters and was a truly radical design. The very small and agile Komet was developed from designs originated by the brilliant Dr Alexander Lippisch, who joined the Messerschmitt company in 1939, having pioneered tailless gliders in the 1920s. The first step toward the revolutionary Me163 was an adaptation of the tailless all-wood DFS 194 research glider, powered by a Walter rocket motor. Fuel for the motor consisted of two hypergolic (spontaneously igniting) liquids, T-Stoff and Z-Stoff, which when mixed reacted violently, the resulting controlled explosion producing around 400kg/882lb of thrust. The rocket-powered glider was test flown at the secret Peenemünde research establishment in June 1940 and the pilot Heini Dittmar reported that the aircraft handled superbly. In later test flights the trailblazing prototype reached 547kph/340mph in level flight and amazed all with its steep climb capability.

The success of the test flights led to six Me163A prototypes, the first of which flew with rocket power in mid-1941. By now the Walter rocket motor had been developed to deliver 750kg/1653lb of thrust, pushing the Komet through the air at 885kph/550mph. One 163A, towed to 4000m/13,125ft before the engine was fired, reached speeds of around 1003kph/623mph (greater than the world speed record of the time) before stability was affected. Minor design changes to the wing eradicated that problem, but others were experienced that plagued the Komet throughout its short service life. Its glider origins resulted in the Komet taking off from a wheeled "dolly", which was jettisoned once the aircraft was off the ground, while for landing the Komet landed on a sprung skid. The take-off and landing phases both held their own hazards for the Komet pilot due to the extremely dangerous nature of the fuels, but the percentage of landing accidents for the Komet, though high, was less than that of the Bf109.

ABOVE: **The revolutionary Komet was certainly the most futuristic form in the sky during World War II.**

The main production version was the Me163B, equipped with a more powerful rocket motor and armed with two 30mm/1.18in cannon in the roots of the swept wooden wings. The Komet first flew in anger on July 28, 1944, when six aircraft of 1/Jagdgeschwader 400 attacked a formation of USAAF Flying Fortresses heading for the Leuna-Merseburg oil refineries. The attack was ineffective as the pilots were not able to bring their guns to bear, mainly due to the very high closing speeds on the targets. At best the Komet pilot could

LEFT: **The Me163 was one of the first combat aircraft with swept wings.** BELOW: **The aircraft took off from a wheeled "dolly" and landed on the skid beneath the aircraft.**

fire his cannon for three seconds before his pass was over and, in addition, the guns only had 60 rounds each.

The preferred method of attack was to take-off when the enemy was known to be nearby, fly above it at very high speed then make a high speed gliding dive on the targets. The maximum period of powered flight was only 7.5 minutes and after the combat the Komet would then make an unpowered glide back to base for a risky landing. The bat-like glider was an absurdly easy target on approach to landing as it could do nothing but land, even if under attack.

The Me163 was used to test an ingenious air-to-air weapon, the SG 500 Jagdfaust (Fighter fist) which consisted of five vertically firing tubes in each wing root. Each tube carried a single 50mm/1.97in shell and all ten would be fired as a salvo when triggered by the shadow of a bomber passing over the Komet, activating a photo-electric cell. All the Komet had to do was fly, top speed, under an enemy aircraft, and the system was proven on April 10, 1945, when a B-17 was destroyed in mid-air by a Jagdfaust-equipped Komet.

In late 1943, Japan negotiated manufacturing rights for the Me163 (as the Mitsubishi J8M1 for the Navy and the Mitsubishi Ki-200 for the Army) but one of the two submarines bringing the technical information to Japan was sunk. With incomplete drawings the Japanese still managed to produce prototypes, one of which flew before the end of the war.

Although around 300 entered service, the Komet never reached its potential and destroyed only nine Allied bombers. It was however by far the most futuristic aircraft in service during World War II.

Messerschmitt Me163B-1a Komet

First flight: June 23, 1943 (powered)
Power: Walter 1700kg/3748lb-thrust HWK 509A-1 rocket motor
Armament: Two 30mm/1.18in cannon
Size: Wingspan – 9.4m/30ft 7.3in
Length – 5.85m/19ft 2.3in
Height – 2.76m/9ft 0.6in
Wing area – 18.5m²/199.1sq ft
Weights: Empty – 1900kg/4190lb
Maximum take-off – 4310kg/9502lb
Performance: Maximum speed – 960kph/596mph
Ceiling – 16,500m/54,000ft
Range – 100km/62 miles or 2 minutes, 30 seconds from top of powered climb
Climb – 5000m/16,400ft per minute

Messerschmitt Me262

The Me262 was Germany's first operational jet aircraft and many Germans believed it was a war-winning aircraft. Design work began on the revolutionary aircraft in late 1938 and power was to be provided by ground-breaking gas turbines under development by BMW. The aircraft was ready before its engines and was test-flown with a single Jumo piston engine in the nose on April 18, 1941. The first test flight with the jet engines installed took place in March 1942. As a safety measure, the piston engine was retained in the nose and the prototype took off under power of all three engines. The two jets seized shortly after take-off and the pilot was lucky to land the aircraft safely. The engines had to be redesigned and the test programme continued with the Me262 powered by two heavier Junkers turbojets. The development of this remarkable aircraft was not considered a top priority by the German High Command and the Messerschmitt company were more concerned with improvements of existing proven combat aircraft such as the Bf109 and Bf110. One of the greatest boosts to the Me262 programme came in May 1943 when legendary Luftwaffe ace General der Jagdflieger (fighter general) Adolf Galland flew the aircraft for the first time. He

ABOVE: **The trailblazing Me262 was the first operational jet aircraft and the Third Reich had high hopes for the futuristic fighter.** LEFT: **On July 25, 1944 the Me262 became the first jet to see combat.**

advocated the mass production of the aircraft as soon as possible but then the whole programme was delayed again by devastating August 1943 Allied bombing raids on the Regensburg factories housing the Me262 production lines. Messerschmitt then moved its jet development operation to Bavaria where a shortage of skilled labour delayed production again by several months. Hitler's oft-quoted ruling that the high-performance aircraft should also be used as a bomber was not the only reason that the 262 entered service late in the war – apart from enemy action, the unreliability and poor performance of the early jet engines were major factors.

And so it was not until July 1944 that the Me262, by now named Schwalbe (swallow), entered front-line service and on July 25 an Me262 became the first jet aircraft used in combat when it attacked a British photo-reconnaissance Mosquito flying over Munich. By late 1944 the Me262 was deployed in three forms – fighter-bomber, pure interceptor and an unarmed reconnaissance version. The first dedicated Me262 interceptor unit went into action for the first time on October 3, 1944. Although it arrived too late to make a real difference to the air war, the 262 was a deadly bomber-killer, equipped with 24 rockets and four 30mm/1.18in cannon. In combat with high-performance P-51 Mustangs, the Me262 sometimes came

LEFT: **Two-seat radar-equipped nightfighter versions were also developed.** BELOW: **Reliability problems plagued the pioneering jet fighter.**

FAR LEFT: **The radical design of the Me262 is evident in this study.** LEFT: **A captured Me262A-1 shipped to Wright Field in the USA for evaluation.**

off worse because of the inferior manoeuvrability compared to the piston-engined aircraft. It was however faster and better armed than the British Meteor jet fighter but the two trailblazing jets never met in air combat.

As a fighter, the German jet scored heavily against Allied bomber formations, but although more than 1400 Me262s were produced by VE Day, less than 300 saw combat as hundreds were destroyed on the ground by Allied bombing. Most stayed firmly on the ground awaiting conversion to bombers or were unable to fly because of lack of fuel, spare parts or trained pilots. The German jet engines were unreliable and engine failures took their toll of the pioneer jet pilots. The under-carriage was prone to collapse and the guns regularly jammed making the pilots vulnerable in a dogfight.

The one period of concerted Me262 fighter activity came during March 18–21, 1945 when some 40 fighter sorties were flown daily against American bombers. It was, however, too little too late.

Although Germany never realized the potential of the 262, this revolutionary aircraft inspired British, American and Soviet designers and directly affected worldwide jet fighter design for years to come.

Messerschmitt Me262A-1a

First flight: July 18, 1942, solely on jet power

Power: Two Junkers 900kg/1984lb thrust Jumo 004B-1 turbojets

Armament: Four 30mm/1.18in cannon in nose plus up to 12 air to-air rockets under each wing

Size: Wingspan – 12.48m/40ft 11.5in
Length – 10.6m/34ft 9.5in
Height – 3.84m/12ft 7in
Wing area – 21.7m^2/233.58sq ft

Weights: Empty – 3800kg/8378lb
Maximum take-off – 6400kg/14,110lb

Performance: Maximum speed – 870kph/540mph
Ceiling – 11450m/37,565ft
Range – 1050km/653 miles
Climb – 1200m/3937ft per minute

Mikoyan-Gurevich MiG-3

The MiG-3 interceptor was the third aircraft designed by Artem Mikoyan and Mikhail Gurevich and was developed from their MiG-1, which first flew in April 1940. The MiG-3 incorporated many improvements over the MiG-1, including a new propeller, a modified wing, greater range, better armour and increased armament. The new MiG was first delivered to front-line units in April 1941 at the same time as the MiG-1, which remained in production despite its short-comings. The Russians knew the MiG-1 was inadequate in many ways but any aircraft were better than none when facing the military might of the Third Reich.

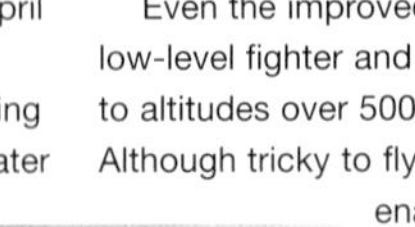

Even the improved MiG-3 was no low-level fighter and was better suited to altitudes over 5000m/16,405ft. Although tricky to fly, the MiG-3's speed enabled it to give the Luftwaffe a real fight for air superiority over the Eastern Front.

Total production of the MiG-1 and -3 amounted to 3422 when MiG-3 production ceased in 1942. By 1942 the latest Luftwaffe fighters were generally getting the better of the long-nosed MiGs, so the type was progressively removed from front-line fighter units during the winter of 1942–3 and went on to be used mainly for armed reconnaissance and close support missions.

Mikoyan-Gurevich MiG-3

First flight: Late 1941
Power: Mikulin 1350hp AM-35A V-12 piston engine
Armament: One 12.7mm/0.5in and two 7.62mm/0.3in machine-guns in nose, plus up to 200kg/441lb of bombs and rockets under wings
Size: Wingspan – 10.2m/33ft 5in
Length – 8.3m/27ft 1in
Height – 3.5m/11ft 6in
Wing area – 17.44m²/187.73sq ft
Weights: Empty – 2595kg/5721lb
Maximum take-off – 3350kg/7385lb
Performance: Maximum speed – 640kph/398mph
Ceiling – 12,000m/39,370ft
Range – 1195km/743 miles
Climb – 1200m/3937ft per minute

LEFT: **The Soviet MiG-3 was a handful for its pilots, but did much to protect the USSR.**
BELOW: **A replica MiG-3 proudly displayed at a museum in Moscow, the city that the type was designed to protect above all else.**

Mitsubishi A5M

The 350kph/217mph top speed specified in a 1934 Imperial Japanese Navy fighter specification seemed to be a tall order at the time. To ease the designers' burden, the need to operate the new fighter from aircraft carriers was not even written into the specification. However, Mitsubishi's offering was the Ka-14, which, having flown in February 1935, showed a top speed of 450kph/280mph. It was designed with minimum drag in mind – the fuselage had a small cross-section, the aluminium skin was flush-riveted and the fixed undercarriage had streamlining spats. It was perhaps too complex a design and the inverted gull-wing that caused some handling headaches was replaced with a more conventional low wing. With this change and powered by a 585hp Kotobuki 2-KAI-1 engine, the type was ordered into production as the Navy Type 96 Carrier Fighter Model 1 (Mitsubishi A5M1) and began to enter service in early 1937. The subsequent A5M2a (basically the same aircraft powered by a 610hp KAI-3 engine) and A5M2b (with the 640hp Kotobuki 3 engine) became the most important Navy fighters during Japan's war with China. Until the A5M2a arrival in theatre, the Japanese were suffering heavy losses but after only a short time the A5M2a achieved total air superiority. Experience of air operations in China speeded up development of the A5M2b, which boasted the luxury of an enclosed cockpit and a three-bladed propeller driven by the more powerful engine. The greenhouse-style canopy was actually unpopular with pilots and was omitted on late-build A5M2bs. The A5M2s were so effective in China that all Chinese air units were withdrawn out of range of the Japanese fighters.

The final, best-known and most numerous production version was the A5M4, which was developed in response to the Chinese withdrawal – greater range was the most important consideration. The A5M4 looked identical to the late-production open-cockpit A5M2bs but was powered by the 710hp Nakajima Kotobuki 41 engine and carried a 160 litre/35.2 gallon drop tank. It entered service in China in 1938 and with its longer range greatly extended the area of Japanese air superiority while driving the less able Chinese air units even further away from the battle area.

ABOVE: **A5M4 of the 14th Kokutai, pictured in 1940.**

Codenamed "Claude" by the Allies, the A5M4 was in front-line use at the start of the Pacific War but it was soon withdrawn for second-line duties (including advanced fighter training) as it was no match for the newer Allied fighters. As the war in the Pacific approached its desperate end, remaining A5M4s were used in kamikaze (divine wind) attacks against Allied ships off the Japanese coast.

Mitsubishi A5M4

First flight: February 4, 1935 (Ka-14)

Power: Nakajima 710hp Kotobuki 41(Bristol Jupiter) nine-cylinder radial piston engine

Armament: Two 7.7mm/0.303in machine-guns firing on each side of upper cylinder of engine, plus two racks for two 30kg/66lb bombs under outer wings

Size: Wingspan – 11m/36ft 1in
Length – 7.55m/24ft 9.25in
Height – 3.2m/10ft 6in
Wing area – 17.8m²/191.6sq ft

Weights: Empty – 1216kg/2681lb
Maximum take-off – 1707kg/3763lb

Performance: Maximum speed – 440kph/273mph
Ceiling – 10,000m/32,800ft
Range – 1200km/746 miles
Climb – 850m/2790ft per minute

Mitsubishi A6M Zero-Sen

Japan's most famous wartime aircraft and the first shipboard fighter capable of beating its land-based opponents had its origins in a 1937 Japanese Navy requirement for a new fighter with a maximum speed exceeding 499kph/310mph to replace the Mitsubishi A5M carrier fighter. The new aircraft had to climb to 3000m/9840ft in 3.5 minutes, and have manoeuvrability and range exceeding any existing fighter together with the impressive armament of two cannon and two machine-guns. Only Mitsubishi accepted the challenge and design work began under the direction of Jiro Horikoshi. The prototype was completed on March 16, 1939, first flew on April 1 and was accepted by the Navy on September 14, 1939 as the A6M1 Carrier Fighter. The chosen powerplant was the lightweight Mitsubishi Zuisei, later replaced by the more powerful Nakajima Sakae (Prosperity) 925hp radial which was only slightly larger and heavier than the original Zuisei. With its new-found power, the fighter amply exceeded the original performance requirements regarded as impossible only a few months earlier. At this time, production models of Navy aircraft were assigned type numbers based on the last number of the current Japanese year in which production began, and as 1940 was the year 2600 in the Japanese calendar, the A6M series was known as the Zero-Sen (Type 00 fighter).

ABOVE: **The A6M Zero-Sen – Japan's finest wartime fighter aircraft.** BELOW: **More Zero-Sens were produced than any other Japanese wartime aircraft.**

Even before the final acceptance of the A6M2 as a production fighter, the Japanese Navy requested that a number of machines be delivered for operational use in China to meet growing aerial resistance. So 15 A6M2s were delivered for service in China and first appeared over Chungking in August 1940 when the new Zeros shot down all the defending Chinese fighters. Washington were informed about the new high-performance Japanese fighter but no heed was taken and so its appearance over Pearl Harbor came as a complete surprise to the American forces. Its subsequent appearance in every major battle area in the opening days of the war seemed to indicate that Japan possessed almost unlimited supplies of the high-performance fighter. In fact in December 1941 the Japanese Navy had well over 400 Zero fighters. In 1941–2 the Zero certainly got the better of all opposing fighters whether it flew from carriers or had to operate over long distances from land bases. During a Japanese carrier-raid on Ceylon (now Sri Lanka), Zeros easily out-turned opposing RAF Hawker Hurricanes, aircraft which until then had been regarded as outstandingly manoeuvrable.

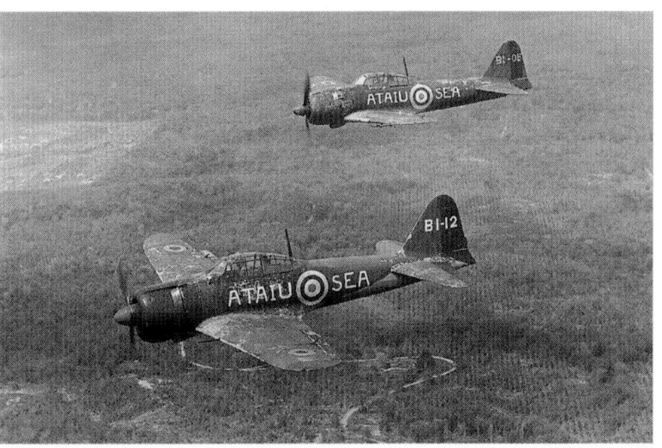

ATOP LEFT: The Zero was of great interest to Japan's enemies. A rare picture of an A6M2 in Chinese Nationalist markings – note the US serviceman by the tail. TOP RIGHT: This A6M3 in USAAF markings was assembled from five Zeros captured by the USA in December 1942. ABOVE LEFT: These captured Zeros pictured in 1946 were evaluated by the RAF in the Far East while flown by Japanese pilots. ABOVE RIGHT: An evaluation A6M3 in USAAF markings pictured over the USA on July 1, 1944.

In mid-1942 the Allies eventually acquired an intact specimen and found that the Zero possessed many shortcomings. It was shipped to the USA where exhaustive tests revealed the fighter's faults and shattered the myth that surrounded it. The tables were turned when the Mitsubishi fighter finally came up against a new generation of US Navy and Army fighters, with powerful engines and heavy protection for their pilot and fuel tanks. Against them the Zero, still basically the design which had flown first in April 1939 offered minimal protection for pilot and fuel tanks and from 1943 the Zeros fell like flies. The installation of the 1560hp Kinsei engine brought the A6M8, the ultimate Zero, closer to the performance of Allied fighters but it was too late. The value of the fighter declined steadily and its lowest point was reached when it was selected as the first aircraft used intentionally as suicide attack (kamikaze or divine-wind) planes. The outstanding success of this form of attack led to the formation of dedicated Kamikaze units, and the bomb-carrying Zeros became the prime suicide attack bombers of the Navy.

More Zero-Sens were produced than any other wartime Japanese aircraft. Mitsubishi alone produced 3879 aircraft of this type, Nakajima built 6,215 which, together with the 844 trainer and floatplane variants produced by Sasebo, Hitachi and Nakajima, brought the grand total of A6M series aircraft to 10,938.

Mitsubishi A6M5 Zero-Sen

First flight: August 1943
Power: Nakajima 1130hp NK1C Sakae 21 14-cylinder two-row radial piston engine
Armament: Two 20mm/0.78in cannon in wing, two 7.7mm/0.303in machine-guns in fuselage, plus two 60kg/132lb bombs on underwing racks
Size: Wingspan – 11m/36ft 1in
Length – 9.06m/29ft 9in Height – 2.98m/9ft 8in
Wing area – 21.3m^2/229.28sq ft
Weights: Empty – 1876kg/4136lb
Maximum take-off – 2733kg/6025lb
Performance: Maximum speed – 570kph/354mph
Ceiling – 11,500m/37,500ft
Range – 1920km/1200 miles with drop tanks
Climb – 6000m/19,685ft in 7.05 minutes

LEFT: **This J2M had clearly seen better days.**

Mitsubishi J2M3 Raiden

First flight: March 20, 1942 (J2M1)
Power: Mitsubishi 1820hp MK4R-A Kasei 23a 14-cylinder two-row radial piston engine
Armament: Four 20mm/0.78in cannon, plus two 60kg/132lb bombs
Size: Wingspan – 10.82m/35ft 5.25in
Length – 9.95m/32ft 7.75in Height – 3.95m/12ft 11.5in Wing area – 20.05m^2/215.82sq ft
Weights: Empty – 2460kg/5423lb
Maximum take-off – 3945kg/8695lb
Performance: Maximum speed – 595kph/370mph
Ceiling – 11,700m/38,385ft
Range – 1055km/655 miles
Climb – 1170m/3838ft per minute

Mitsubishi J2M Raiden

The J2M, designed by the same team as the Zero, was the Japanese Navy's first interceptor, being designed to operate from shore bases to destroy enemy bombers. Breaking with the Japanese tradition of manoeuvrability above all else, the Raiden (thunderbolt) was built for speed and climb. Among the design points of interest were a streamlined nose, retractable tailwheel and a laminar flow wing with "combat" flaps for improved agility. The small aerodynamic nose was achieved by connecting the propeller to the engine (which was set further back in the fuselage) by an extension shaft. Early J2M1 versions flew in March 1942 but proved troublesome and did not meet the Navy's requirements, consequently an improved Kasei 23a-engined J2M2 was ordered for production in October 1942. Continued technical difficulties meant the aircraft did not enter service until December 1943 and then as the improved J2M3 version with four wing-mounted cannon.

Codenamed "Jack" by the Allies, the Raiden played a key role in the defence of the Japanese homeland in the closing months of World War II.

LEFT: **A captured Ki-46 with US markings.**

Mitsubishi Ki-46-III Kai

First flight: October 1944
Power: Mitsubishi 1500hp Ha-112II piston engines
Armament: Two 20mm/0.78in cannon in nose and one 37mm/1.46in oblique forward-firing cannon in upper fuselage
Size: Wingspan – 14.7m/48ft 2.75in
Length – 11.48m/37ft 8.25in
Height – 3.88m/12ft 8.75in
Wing area – 32m^2/344.46sq ft
Weights: Empty – 3831kg/8446lb
Maximum take-off – 6228kg/13730lb
Performance: Maximum speed – 630kph/391mph
Ceiling – 10,500m/34,450ft
Range – 2000km/1243 miles
Climb – 600m/1970ft per minute

Mitsubishi Ki-46-III Kai

As Japan was forced on the defensive by the Allies, the Imperial Staff recognized the need for heavy fighter-interceptors to defend against Allied bombers. Since the very high-performance Ki-46 reconnaissance aircraft was some 83kph/53mph faster than the Army's standard twin-engine fighter (the Ki-45), the Ki-46 was selected for development as a stop-gap high-altitude interceptor. The development work, carried out by the Army Aerotechnical Research Institute, began in June 1943.

Photographic equipment was removed from the nose and replaced by two forward-firing 20mm/0.78in cannon, complemented by an obliquely forward-firing 37mm/1.46in cannon in the upper fuselage. Around 200 interceptor versions were built.

The aircraft appeared from October 1944 and saw service in November, but proved disappointing against B-29 daylight raids mainly due to its climb rate. When B-29 gunners found their mark, the Ki-46 was very vulnerable because of its lack of armour and self-sealing fuel tanks.

When the American bombers switched to night operations the Ki-46 proved to be even less effective as it was never fitted with radar for operational use.

Mitsubishi Ki-109

In 1943 the B-29 Superfortress was causing great concern among the Japanese military. The new super-bomber would have to be stopped and one of the means considered was a bomber hunter-killer developed from the fast and agile Mitsubishi Ki-67 heavy bomber. Initial plans called for a hunter version equipped with radar and a powerful searchlight that would have operated in concert with a killer version that would have destroyed the enemy aircraft. The scheme was then simplified to a large-calibre cannon-armed day interceptor.

The main offensive armament was a manually loaded 75mm/2.95in anti-aircraft cannon that could be fired out of range of the B-29's defending guns. The first prototype was completed in August 1944, two months after the dreaded B-29s carried out their first bombing raid on Japan.

Production versions had improved engines over the original bomber version and the sole defensive armament was a 12.7mm/0.5in machine-gun in the tail turret. Although it still lacked high-altitude performance, 22 examples of the highly manoeuvrable Ki-109s entered service, but by then the B-29s had switched to low-level night operations anyway.

TOP: **The Ki-109 was developed from the Ki-67 heavy bomber. Two versions were originally planned to work as a team – one radar-equipped hunter and a heavily armed killer. Only the armed version appeared.** ABOVE: **The Ki-109 differed from the Ki-67 pictured by mounting a 75mm/3in cannon in the nose.**

Mitsubishi Ki-109

First flight: August 1944
Power: Two Mitsubishi 1900hp Ha-104 piston engines
Armament: One 75mm/2.95in cannon in nose and one 12.7mm/0.5in machine-gun in tail
Size: Wingspan – 22.5m/73ft 9.75in
Length – 17.95m/58ft 10.75in
Height – 5.8m/19ft 1in
Wing area – 65.85m²/708.8sq ft
Weights: Empty – 7424kg/16367lb
Maximum take-off – 10,800kg/23,810lb
Performance: Maximum speed – 550kph/342mph
Ceiling – 9470m/31,070ft
Range – 2200km/1367 miles
Climb – 450m/1476ft per minute

Morane-Saulnier M.S.406

Morane-Saulnier built the 406 in response to a 1934 French Air Ministry requirement for a single-seat fighter. It first flew in August 1935 and was unusual for its Plymax construction – plywood with a light alloy sheet glued to the outside made up most of the aircraft except for the fabric-covered rear fuselage. Although the aircraft had a retractable undercarriage, it also had a tail-skid instead of a tailwheel.

The design was thoroughly tested by the M.S.405 series of pre-production aircraft, and in March 1938 Morane-Saulnier got an order for 1000 examples of the production M.S.406C-1, the first of which flew in January 1939. Export orders were secured from China, Finland, Lithuania, Turkey, Poland and Yugoslavia. Swiss acquisition of two early examples led to the licence-built EFW D-3800 versions in that country.

Production problems with the 12Y engine meant that only 572 completed aircraft had been delivered to the French Air Force by the time war broke out. The brave French pilots soon found that their fighters, though only six years old as a design, were from an earlier age compared to the Messerschmitts that they had to fight. More than 400 M.S.406s were lost against 175 enemy aircraft in the Battle of France.

Although deliveries continued to the French Air Force and over 1000 had been delivered by the fall of France, only one group of the Vichy French Air Force operated the M.S.406 after the armistice.

ABOVE: **The M.S.406's fuselage is reminiscent of the Hawker Hurricane.** BELOW: **A row of M.S.406s of the Polish Air Force.**

Morane-Saulnier M.S.406

First flight: August 8, 1935
Power: Hispano-Suiza 860hp 12Y-31 V-12 liquid-cooled engine
Armament: One 20mm/0.78in cannon firing through propeller hub and two 7.5mm/0.295in machine-guns in wings
Size: Wingspan – 10.6m/34ft 9.75in
Length – 8.16m/26ft 9.25in
Height – 2.83m/9ft 3.75in
Wing area – 16m²/172.23sq ft
Weights: Empty – 1900kg/4189lb
Maximum take-off – 2470kg/5445lb
Performance: Maximum speed – 485kph/302mph
Ceiling – 9400m/30,840ft
Range – 800km/497 miles
Climb – 850m/2789ft per minute

Morane-Saulnier Type N

The Type N, nicknamed "Bullet" by the Royal Flying Corps, was a neat little mid-wing monoplane that became the first French fighter aircraft – the British used the type due to the shortage of good British fighting scouts at the time. It first flew in July 1914, with the famous French pilot Roland Garros at the controls.

A huge metal propeller spinner, designed to streamline the front of the aircraft, earned the Type N its nickname but also caused engines to overheat because it so effectively deflected air around the aircraft instead of over the engine. As a result the spinner was often deleted from 1915 and in fact caused little loss of performance.

The N was armed with a fixed machine-gun, but without a synchronization gear, as the Allies had yet to develop it. Instead the N used metal bullet-deflectors on the propeller blades, an installation pioneered by Garros on a Type L. This technique was far from ideal as the impact of the bullets on the deflectors could still shatter the propeller or weaken the engine mount with disastrous results. There were also occasional ricochets of the bullets back at the pilot. With a high, for the time, landing speed, the Type N was a handful and required a skilful pilot at the controls.

The Type N was less popular than the earlier Morane-Saulnier Type L Parasol and as the Type N did not do well against the Fokker Eindecker, only 49 were built in 1917. In spite of that, the RFC Type Ns saw plenty of action as did those that flew with the French and the Russians.

At that point in aviation history, aircraft development proceeded so fast that most fighter planes were virtually obsolete by the time they reached the front-line squadrons.

Morane-Saulnier Type N

First flight: July 1914
Power: Le Rhône 110hp 9C rotary piston engine
Armament: One fixed forward-firing 7.7 or 8mm/0.303 or 0.315in machine-gun
Size: Wingspan – 8.3m/27ft 2.75in
Length – 6.7m/21ft 11.75in
Height – 2.5m/8ft 2.5in
Wing area – $11m^2$/118.41sq ft
Weights: Empty – 288kg/635lb
Maximum take-off – 444kg/979lb
Performance: Maximum speed – 165kph/102.5mph
Ceiling – 4000m/13,123ft
Range – 225km/140 miles
Climb – 250m/820ft per minute

LEFT: **Complete with huge spinner, the Type N experienced engine overheating problems.**
BELOW: **The earlier M.S Type L Parasol.**
BOTTOM: **With the spinner removed, the Type N experienced no further overheating problems.**

Nakajima Ki-27

The Nakajima Ki-27 was derived from a private venture all-metal stressed-skin aircraft called the PE designed by Nakajima in 1935. When the company was invited by the Imperial Japanese Army to tender a design for an advanced fighter, a revised PE was submitted as the Ki-27.

The prototype made its first flight in October 1936 and was accepted by the Army, after comparative trials with other prototypes, in December 1937. It was called the Army Type 97 Fighter Model A – the 97 refers to the year it went into service which was the Japanese year 2597. The Ki-27 was the Imperial Japanese Army's first monoplane fighter but it had fixed landing gear. The fighter was basic in many ways – it had a skid instead of a heavier tailwheel, no pilot armour or self-sealing fuel tanks, nor did it have a starter motor. This left the aircraft very light and incredibly manoeuvrable.

The Ki-27, codenamed "Nate" by the Allies, made its combat début over northern China in early 1938 and retained air superiority until the Chinese deployed the Polikarpov I-16. Nates later took part in the invasion of Burma, Malaya and the Philippines.

At the outbreak of the Pacific War most front-line Japanese fighter units were equipped with the Ki-27 and the type did prove to be initially very effective against the Allies, but once they were pitched against the more modern Western fighters, they were withdrawn to the Japanese mainland where they served until 1943. Nates did however continue in Japanese service in Manchuria until the end of World War II. Home-based examples were also used as advanced trainers and even as Kamikaze aircraft.

Nakajima Ki-27a

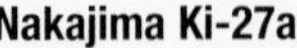

First flight: October 15, 1936
Power: Nakajima 710hp Ha-1b air-cooled radial piston engine
Armament: Two 7.7mm/0.303in machine-guns in nose
Size: Wingspan – 11.31m/37ft 1.5in
Length – 7.53m/24ft 8.5in
Height – 3.25m/10ft 8in
Wing area – 18.55m²/199.68sq ft
Weights: Empty – 1110kg/2447lb
Maximum take-off – 1790kg/3946lb
Performance: Maximum speed – 470kph/292mph
Ceiling – 12,250m/40190ft
Range – 635km/389 miles
Climb – 900m/2953ft per minute

LEFT: **The first monoplane fighter of the Imperial Japanese Army, the Ki-27.** BELOW: **The Ki-27 was a very basic light fighter equipped with a tail skid in place of a tailwheel.**

Nakajima Ki-43 Hayabusa

In 1937, when the Japanese Imperial Army decided to acquire a fighter with a retractable undercarriage to succeed the Ki-27, it turned to the Nakajima company for a replacement, which emerged as the Ki-43 Hayabusa (peregrine falcon). Like the Ki-27 before it, lightness and manoeuvrability were central to the design of the Ki-43 so it had no pilot armour, self-sealing fuel tanks or starter motor. It was, however, disappointing in flight tests during early 1939 and development was abandoned until spring 1941, when combat flaps were added, thus increasing the wing area as required and creating a fighter that could turn inside the highly manoeuvrable Zero. This modified version, which could dogfight with the best of the Allies' fighters, went into service in June 1941 and proved very successful despite its light armament. Most of Japan's Army fighter aces built up their scores while flying the Ki-43.

After encounters with the newer Allied fighters, armour and self-sealing fuel tanks were added, together with a more powerful engine to produce the II version, a clipped-wing variant of which was widely produced. The Ki-43 was in action throughout the Pacific theatre in World War II and in the final days was used in the defence of Tokyo and for kamikaze (divine wind) missions. Almost 6000 were built in all – this aeroplane, codenamed "Oscar" by the Allies, was deployed in greater numbers than any other Imperial Army fighter and was second only to the Navy's Zero in terms of sheer numbers in the Japanese inventory.

As an interesting post-war footnote, in late 1945 the French Armeé de l'Air flew captured Oscars painted in French markings in the ground support role against Viet Minh forces in Indochina. Captured Hayabusas were also operated by the Indonesian People's Security Forces against the Dutch in the same period.

ABOVE: **The Ki-43 was in service throughout the war in the Pacific.** LEFT: **A Ki-43-II captured by the Allies before the end of World War II, rebuilt for evaluation.**

Nakajima Ki-43-II Hayabusa

First flight: January 1939
Power: Nakajima 1150hp Ha-115 air-cooled radial piston engine
Armament: Two 12.7mm/0.5in synchronized machine-guns, plus two 30kg/66lb or 250kg/551lb bombs
Size: Wingspan – 10.84m/35ft 6.75in
Length – 8.92m/29ft 3.3in
Height – 3.27m/10ft 8.75in
Wing area – 21.4m^2/230.4sq ft
Weights: Empty – 1910kg/4211lb
Maximum take-off – 2925kg/6450lb
Performance: Maximum speed – 530kph/329mph
Ceiling – 11,200m/36,750ft
Range – 1760km/1095 miles
Climb – 5000m/16,405ft in 5 minutes, 49 seconds

Nakajima Ki-44 Shoki

The Ki-44 was designed purely as an interceptor, so high speed and good climb were sought at the expense of manoeuvrability. The type first flew in August 1940 and when tested against an imported Messerschmitt Bf109E was shown to be superior in performance.

The Shoki (demon) did not enter production until mid-1942 and finally reached a production total of 1225. Virtually all were used in the defence of the Japanese home islands and in one defensive mission on February 19, 1945 a small number of Shokis attacked a force of 120 B-29s, destroying ten of the US bombers. The Allied codename for the Ki-44 was "Tojo".

TOP: **The Shoki was a good fighter, but high landing speeds demanded respect for the type from its pilots.** ABOVE: **The Allied codename for the Ki-44 was "Tojo".** LEFT: **Total production of the Ki-44 exceeded 1200.** BELOW: **The Ki-44 was an effective interceptor that could have wreaked havoc among enemy bomber formations, had it been deployed effectively in sufficient numbers.**

Nakajima Ki-44-IIb Shoki

First flight: August 1940
Power: Nakajima 1520hp Ha-109 radial piston engine
Armament: Four forward-firing 12.7mm/0.5in machine-guns
Size: Wingspan – 9.45m/31ft
Length – 8.8m/28ft 10.5in
Height – 3.25m/10ft 8in
Wing area – $15m^2$/161.46sq ft
Weights: Empty – 2105kg/4641lb
Maximum take-off – 2995kg/6603lb
Performance: Maximum speed – 605kph/376mph
Ceiling – 11,200m/36,745ft
Range – 1700km/1056 miles
Climb – 1200m/3940ft per minute

ABOVE LEFT: **A Ki-84 of the 11th Sentai.** ABOVE: **The Ki-84 was a formidable fighter aircraft with an excellent performance.**

Nakajima Ki-84 Hayate

Introduced in mid-1944, the Nakajima Ki-84 Hayate (gale) was numerically the most important fighter that served with the Japanese Army Air Force during the last year of the war in the Pacific. If it had been available in larger numbers earlier in the war, the Hayate could have been a major obstacle for Allied aircraft to overcome. It was the equal of the most advanced Allied fighters including the P-51 and P-47 and in many cases had better climb and manoeuvrability. Japan was so desperate for Ki-84s in the last months of the war that underground factories were being built with a planned output of 200 aircraft per month.

The Ki-84 began in 1942 when the Nakajima Aeroplane Co. began to design a replacement for its Ki-43 Hayabusa. The JAAF wanted a high-performance long-range fighter that could outperform those of the Allies.

The Ki-84 prototype flew for the first time in March 1943 and was quickly shown to be the best-performing Japanese fighter aircraft then available for production.

Service tests of the Ki-84 began in Japan under operational conditions in October 1943 and the type was accepted for production as the Army Type 4 Fighter Model 1A Hayate (gale) or Ki-84-Ia.

Production aircraft began to roll off the assembly lines in April 1944. In March 1944 the experimental squadron that was conducting the service test trials of the Ki-84 was disbanded, and its personnel transferred to the 22nd Sentai which was re-equipped with production Hayates and transferred to China in August 1944 for combat against the USAAF's 14th Air Force. The Ki-84-Ia swiftly established itself as a formidable foe that compared very well with the best Allied fighters of the time.

The Hayate exhibited an excellent performance and climb rate, and unlike most earlier Japanese fighters, it was well armoured for pilot protection.

The Ki-84 proved faster than the P-51D Mustang and the P-47D Thunderbolt at all but the highest altitudes while at medium height the Hayate was so fast that it was virtually uncatchable.

Fighter-bomber versions of the Ki-84 also proved to be formidable combat aircraft. On April 15, 1945 a flight of 11 Hayates made a surprise air attack on American airfields on Okinawa damaging or destroying many aircraft on the ground.

The Hayate did have some handling idiosyncrasies. Taxiing and ground handling were generally hazardous and on take-off, the considerable engine torque caused a swing to port once the tail came up.

Most Ki-84 defects were simply due to poor quality control in a country under siege. Later examples had progressively poorer performance and mechanical reliability – the metal of the landing gear struts inadequately hardened during manufacture, which made them likely to snap on landing. Production of the aircraft never reached the desired levels because the Nakajima factory was regularly bombed by US B-29 Superfortresses.

ABOVE: **This Hayate was shipped to Wright Field in the USA for post-war evaluation by the USAAF.**

Nakajima Ki-84-Ia Hayate

First flight: March 1943

Power: Nakajima 1900hp Ha-45 radial piston engine

Armament: Two 12.7mm/0.5in machine-guns plus two 20mm/0.78in cannon and two underwing 250kg/551lb bombs

Size: Wingspan – 11.24m/36ft 10.5in
Length – 9.92m/32ft 6.5in
Height – 3.39m/11ft 1.5in
Wing area – 21m^2/226sq ft

Weights: Empty – 2660kg/5864lb
Maximum take-off – 3890kg/8576lb

Performance: Maximum speed – 631kph/392mph
Ceiling – 10,500m/34,350ft
Range – 2168km/1347 miles
Climb – 1100m/3600ft per minute

Nieuport fighting scouts

The Nieuport fighting scouts earned a fine reputation for both their designer Gustave Delage and the company that built them. The Nieuport XI was developed from the 1914 Bébé racer aircraft and retained the earlier aircraft's name as a nickname. By the summer of 1915 the first Bébés were in service in France and the Dardanelles with Britain's Royal Flying Corps and Royal Naval Air Service and were one of the first true fighters used by the British. In the hands of an experienced pilot, the tiny Nieuport XI had no problem outmanoeuvring an Eindecker and bringing it down. Powered by an 80hp Gnome or Le Rhône engine, the aircraft were much better than what was in use at the time. They were highly agile fighters with good rates of climb and speed but the chief problem lay in the fragility of the wing structure which could fail in flight.

They were armed with a single Hotchkiss or Lewis machine-gun mounted on the top wing but the Nieuport XI could also carry eight Le Prieur rockets for attacking balloons. In addition to French production, the Nieuport XI was also built in Russia, Spain and the Netherlands, as well as being copied by German designers.

Nieuport XI

First flight: Early 1915
Power: Le Rhône 80hp 9C rotary piston engine
Armament: One 7.7mm/0.303in Lewis gun
Size: Wingspan – 7.55m/24ft 9in
Length – 5.8m/19ft 0.75in
Height – 2.45m/8ft 0.5in
Wing area – 13m²/139.94sq ft
Weights: Empty – 350kg/772lb
Maximum take-off – 480kg/1058lb
Performance: Maximum speed – 155kph/97mph
Ceiling – 4500m/14,765ft
Range – 2 hours, 30 minutes endurance
Climb – about 200m/660ft per minute

ABOVE: **The Nieuports were one of the most successful "families" of World War I aircraft.** BELOW AND BOTTOM: **The Nieuport XI was one of the earliest fighter aircraft used by Britain's RFC and RNAS. Though manoeuvrable, the type's wings were fragile.**

The Nieuport XVII was one of the most famous fighter aircraft of World War I and was a significant improvement on the Bébé. The type first appeared with the French on the Western Front in May 1916, and was a direct development of the XI. It had a more powerful engine, larger wings and a stiffening of the entire structure. It first had the 110hp Le Rhône 9J rotary engine, and then was upgraded to the more powerful 130hp Clerget 9B. The XVII combined outstanding manoeuvrability with good speed and excellent climb, and influenced the design of many other aircraft – the German Siemens-Schuckert DI was, except for the tailplane, a direct copy of it.

Reloading of the top wing gun on this model was made easier by the Foster gun mount, a curved metal rail along which the gun could be pulled back and down – the pilot could then reach the magazine on top of the machine-gun but this was a difficult feat in anything but straight and level flight. Nevertheless many World War I Allied aces flew these aircraft, including René Fonck, Georges Guynemer, Charles Nungesser, Albert Ball and Billy Bishop.

The Nieuport 28 first flew in June 1917 and was the first fighter aircraft flown in combat by pilots of the American Expeditionary Forces (AEF) in World War I. Its second armed patrol with an AEF unit on April 14, 1918 resulted in two victories when Lts Alan Winslow and Douglas Campbell (the first American-trained ace) of the 94th Aero Squadron each downed an enemy aircraft. The 28 was very different to the earlier Nieuports and lost the familiar slim lower wing in favour of a lower wing almost as large as the top one.

By the time the Nieuport 28 was in service it had been overtaken in terms of performance by the SPAD, but American pilots maintained a good ratio of kills to losses while flying the Nieuport. The Nieuport was more manoeuvrable than the sturdier SPAD XIII that replaced it, but had a reputation for fragility and a tendency, in a dive, to shed the fabric covering its upper wing. Even so, many American aces of World War I, including Eddie Rickenbacker with 26 victories, flew the French-built Nieuport 28. Post-war, many Nieuport 28s continued to fly in air forces around the world.

Nieuport XVII

First flight: January 1916
Power: Le Rhône 120hp rotary piston engine
Armament: One 7.7mm/0.303in Lewis gun on flexible top wing mount plus one 7.7m/0.303in synchronized machine-gun
Size: Wingspan – 8.2m/26ft 10.75in
Length – 5.96m/19ft 7in
Height – 2.44m/8ft
Wing area – 14.75m²/158.77sq ft
Weights: Empty – 374kg/825lb
Maximum take-off – 560kg/1235lb
Performance: Maximum speed – 170kph/106mph
Ceiling – 5350m/17,550ft
Range – 250km/155 miles
Climb – 4000m/13,125ft in 19 minutes, 30 seconds

ABOVE: **Around 90 examples of the 120hp or 130hp engined Nieuport 27 were in service briefly with the RFC from mid-1917 to April 1918.** BELOW: **The ultimate Nieuport – the 28. As well as extensive wartime service, the type was also widely used post-World War I.**

Nieuport 28

First flight: June 14, 1917
Power: Gnome 160hp 9N rotary piston engine
Armament: Two fixed 7.7mm/0.303in machine-guns
Size: Wingspan – 8m/26ft 3in
Length – 6.2m/20ft 4in
Height – 2.48m/8ft 1.75in
Wing area – 20m²/215.29sq ft
Weights: Empty – 532kg/1172lb
Maximum take-off – 740kg/1631lb
Performance: Maximum speed – 195kph/121mph
Ceiling – 5200m/17,060ft
Range – 400km/248 miles
Climb – 5000m/16,405ft in 21 minutes, 15 seconds

North American P/F-51 Mustang

Considered to be one of the greatest US fighters ever, the first Mustangs were actually designed and built in the United States with Allison engines to a British specification for the Royal Air Force. Designed and built in the remarkably short time of 117 days, the new fighter was test flown in October 1940. The Mustang could outperform contemporary American fighters but the Allison's lack of power in the climb and at altitude led to the early Mustang's use in the European theatre being limited to armed tactical reconnaissance. In October 1942 RAF Mustangs attacked targets on the Dortmund-Ems canal and became the first British single-engined aircraft over Germany in World War II. The A-36 Invader was the dedicated dive-bomber version of the early Mustang and equipped the USAAF in Sicily, where it was used to devastating effect.

When in 1942 the Mustang airframe was matched with the proven Rolls-Royce Merlin, the "Cadillac of the skies" was born and the P-51 Mustang became one of the most successful fighter aircraft of all time. In October 1943, as a result of unacceptable losses, unescorted US daylight bomber

ABOVE: With its long range, the P-51 Mustang enabled the resumption of US bombing missions deep in enemy territory. BELOW: This preserved P-51 is painted as the personal aircraft of US wartime ace Clarence "Bud" Anderson.

missions deep into enemy Europe were suspended. No Allied fighter had the range to defend and escort the American bombers all the way to the target. The arrival of the Mustang, with its US-built Merlin engines and droppable wing tanks enabled the bombers to resume their daylight missions, safe in the knowledge that their "little buddies" could fly with them all the way to Berlin and back. Even at that range, the P-51's performance was superior to that of its Luftwaffe adversaries. The Mustang allowed the Allies to gain command of the daylight sky over Germany and as a result made a major contribution to the defeat of Nazi Germany.

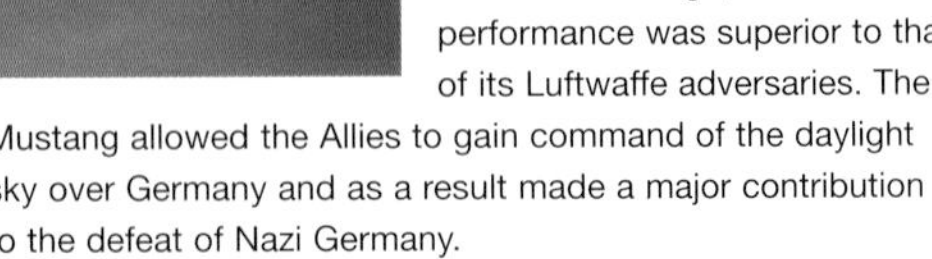

The Mustang was a very comfortable long-range aircraft and pilot visibility was excellent. Cockpit ergonomics were well thought out, with everything readily to hand. It was so aerodynamically clean that it was capable of higher speeds than

Spitfires fitted with the same engine. Although manoeuvrable it demanded, however, great physical effort from the pilot to get the best from the aircraft at high speed.

The P-51D was produced in greater numbers than any other model but improvements continued to be made to the design, culminating in the P-51H, which was 454kg/1000lb lighter than the D model and was the fastest Allied piston-engined aircraft of the war.

Total production amounted to 15,586 and after World War II the Mustang was operated by at least 55 air forces, making it the world's most widely used fighter at the time. Licence-built versions were also produced in Australia in the late 1940s.

Always thought of as a World War II fighter, the P-51 was in action for many years after 1945. Mothballed USAF P/F-51s returned to service for the Korean War as fighter-bombers and also scored a number of air-to-air victories. South African and Australian Mustangs also served in the conflict until being replaced by jets.

Dutch P-51Ds and Ks were in combat in the Dutch East Indies in 1946 and following the withdrawal of Dutch forces the P-51s were given over to the embryonic Indonesian Air Force, who operated the type into the 1970s. The Israeli Air Force fielded Mustangs during the 1956 Arab-Israeli conflict and on January 15, 1962 Indonesian F-51Ds provided top cover for a failed attempt to invade Dutch New Guinea. Dutch Hawker Hunter F. Mk 4s were ready to engage the Mustangs when negotiations halted what could have been a remarkable air combat episode.

Such was the quality and longevity of the original design that the P-51 was put back into production in 1967 as a turboprop-powered counter-insurgency aircraft.

TOP: The Cadillac of the skies – looking every inch a thoroughbred. ABOVE: Where it all began – a Mustang I of No.2 Squadron RAF. Due to the low altitude power ratings of the Allison engines installed, the type was initially limited to armed tactical reconnaissance. BELOW: Drop tanks gave the Mustang even longer legs, and helped the type regain control of the sky over Europe from the Luftwaffe.

North American P-51D Mustang

First flight: October 26, 1940

Power: Packard 1590hp V-1650-7 Merlin piston engine

Armament: Six 12.7mm/0.5in machine-guns and up to 454kg/1000lb of bombs or rockets in place of drop tanks

Size: Wingspan – 11.29m/37ft
Length – 9.85m/32ft 3in
Height – 4.16m/13ft 8in
Wing area – 21.83m^2/235sq ft

Weights: Empty – 3230kg/7125lb
Maximum take-off – 5262kg/11,600lb

Performance: Maximum speed – 703kph/437mph
Ceiling – 12,771m/41,900ft
Range – 3347km/2080 miles with drop tanks
Climb – 1060m/3475ft per minute

Northrop P/F-61 Black Widow

The large and heavily armed twin-engine twin-boom Black Widow was the first ever aircraft specifically designed as a nightfighter and was built to meet a specification issued in October 1940, following the early successes of RAF nightfighters against the Luftwaffe. In the nose it carried the then new radar equipment, which enabled its crew to locate enemy aircraft in total darkness and manoeuvre into an attacking position. The XP-61 was flight-tested in 1942 and delivery of production aircraft began in late 1943, following hold-ups due to technical challenges of both aircraft and radar that had to be overcome.

The P-61A flew its first operational intercept missions as a nightfighter in Europe in July 1944 and destroyed four German bombers in the type's first engagement. Black Widows were also credited with the destruction of nine V-1 flying bombs in Europe. Meanwhile in the Pacific, a Black Widow claimed its first kill on the night of July 6–7, 1944. As the P-61s became available, they replaced the stop-gap Douglas P-70s in all USAAF nightfighter squadrons.

Armament was carried below the nose and in a remotely controlled barbette at top centre of the fuselage – the latter was deleted early in production of the A model due to buffeting problems when pointed at right angles to the aircraft's centre line. The dorsal barbette was later reinstated during production of the B-model, which differed from the A model by being 20.3cm/8in longer and having the ability to carry four 726kg/1600lb bombs or 1136 litre/300 US gallon drop tanks. 200 P-61As were built, while B model production reached 450. After feedback about the P-61's combat performance, the P-61C was developed, powered by turbo-supercharged R-2800-73 engines with an emergency output of 2800hp apiece. As the take-off weight of the type increased to 18,144kg/40,000lb, a recommended take-off run of 4.8km/3 miles was required.

A number of Black Widows continued to serve until 1950 in USAF service (by then designated F-51s) and in 1949 were the first aircraft of the embryonic US Air Defense Command, founded to defend the USA from Soviet air attack.

Northrop P-61B Black Widow

First flight: May 21, 1942 (XP-61)
Power: Two Pratt & Whitney 2000hp R-2800-65 Double Wasp 18-cylinder radial piston engines
Armament: Four 12.7mm/0.5in machine-guns in upper turret, four 20mm/0.78in cannons in belly, plus up to 2905kg/6400lb of bombs
Size: Wingspan – 20.11m/66ft 0.75in
Length – 15.11m/49ft 7in
Height – 4.47m/14ft 8in
Wing area – 61.53m²/662.36sq ft
Weights: Empty – 10,637kg/23,450lb
Maximum take-off – 16,420kg/36,200lb
Performance: Maximum speed – 589kph/366mph
Ceiling – 10,060m/33,000ft
Range – 2172km/1350 miles
Climb – 637m/2090ft per minute

BELOW: **The P-61 Black Widow was the first ever purpose-designed nightfighter, and proved the value of the dedicated nightfighter aircraft.**

Petlyakov Pe-3

Originally designed as a high altitude interceptor (designated VI-100), the Pe-2 became one of the most significant aircraft in the wartime Allied inventory. The prototype flew in mid-1939 and its high speed and high altitude capability would indeed have made it a very effective interceptor. However, early in 1940 the decision was taken to develop the type as a bomber as a priority over a high flying interceptor. It performed outstandingly as a tactical/dive-bomber and was very fast for the time. Two RAF Hurricane squadrons were sent to Russia in the autumn of 1941 to strengthen the Soviet defences, and when escorting the Pe-2 on bombing missions found it very hard to keep up.

When an early Pe-2 dive-bomber was modified as a multi-role fighter prototype it was given the designation Pe-3. It first flew in early 1941 and was structurally similar to the bomber version. The fighter had a two-man crew (as opposed to three for the bomber) and they sat back to back with the observer gunner facing backwards. Additional fuel was carried in the main bomb bay and the small bomb bays in the rear of the two engine nacelles. Only 23 examples were built prior to the German invasion of Russia at which point production ceased.

The Pe-2 did however make it into production as a fighter in the summer of 1941. Every second aircraft on the Pe-2 production line was hastily modified to fighter configuration and were designated Pe-3bis. Armament consisted of two 20mm/0.78in cannon carried in the bomb bay. The bomber's nose armament of two 7.62mm/0.31in machine-guns were sometimes replaced by two harder-hitting 12.7mm/0.5in cannon, while the bomber's 12.7mm/0.5in cannon in the dorsal turret was retained. Front-line units had deliveries from August 1941 and those aircraft used in the nightfighter role were equipped with special equipment. Around 300 aircraft were built in all.

TOP: **The Pe-3 bristled with offensive armament.** ABOVE: **From mid-1941, every alternate Pe-2 on the production line was made as a fighter.**

Petlyakov Pe-3bis

First flight: December 22, 1939 (VI-100 prototype)
Power: Two Klimov 1260hp VK-105PF V12 piston engines
Armament: Two 20mm/0.78in cannon in bomb bay, two 7.62mm/0.31in machine-guns or two 12.7mm/0.5in cannon in nose, plus one 12.7mm/0.5in cannon in dorsal turret
Size: Wingspan – 17.16m/56ft 3.6in
Length – 12.6m/41ft 4.5in
Height – 3.42m/11ft 2.6in
Wing area – 40.5m^2/435.95sq ft
Weights: Empty – 5870kg/12,941lb
Maximum take-off – 8040kg/17,725lb
Performance: Maximum speed – 530kph/329mph
Ceiling – 8800m/28,700ft
Range – 1700km/1056 miles
Climb – 5000m/16,405ft in 10 minutes, 12 seconds

Pfalz D.III

The D.III appeared in mid-1917 and was built with the experience gained by Pfalz while producing LFG-Roland fighters. The D.III biplane fighter, the design of which owed much to the LFG-Roland D.I and D.II, was a competent, agile fighter aircraft that was also strong, easy to fly and popular with pilots. About 600 were built and supplied at least at first, only to Bavarian fighter units in the German Air Force – this was no doubt due to the fact that the Pfalz factory was run by the Bavarian government. The excellent Pfalz D.XII was a development of the D.III and was, in 1918, accepted by the German High Command for mass production.

Among the refinements was the removal of the radiator from the top wing to the engine to prevent unfortunate pilots from being scalded by a punctured cooling system. Although the D.XII was powered by the same Mercedes engine as the D.III, it had a slightly higher top speed than the earlier mark.

ABOVE: **D.XIIs were in action on the Western Front from October 1918, but could do little to affect the final outcome of World War I.**

ABOVE: **A Pfalz D.IIIa. By the end of 1917 some 275 were in action at the Front, but by April 1918 this number had risen to 433.**

Pfalz D.IIIa

First flight: Summer 1917
Power: Mercedes 180hp D.IIIa in-line piston engine
Armament: Two fixed 7.92mm/0.31in machine-guns
Size: Wingspan – 9.4m/30ft 10in
Length – 6.95m/22ft 9.5in
Height – 2.67m/8ft 9in
Wing area – 22.1m^2/237.89sq ft
Weights: Empty – 695kg/1532lb
Maximum take-off – 935kg/2061lb
Performance: Maximum speed – 165kph/103mph
Ceiling – 5180m/17,000ft
Range – 2 hours, 30 minutes endurance
Climb – 250m/820ft per minute

Polikarpov I-15

LEFT: **The I-15 fought from Manchuria to Spain.**

Developed from the earlier I-5 fighter, the agile little Polikarpov I-15 biplane actually replaced the monoplane I-16 in service in parts of the USSR. Having first flown during October 1933 in prototype TsKB-3 form, production of the I-15 Chaika (gull) began in 1934 and continued for three years.

The I-15 was used extensively by the Republicans during the Spanish Civil War (1936–9) and earned the nickname "Chato", meaning flat-nosed. The first I-15s arrived in Spain during October 1936 and during the subsequent combats earned a reputation as a tough opponent. In addition to the imported examples, Spanish government factories also licence-built some 287 examples and many fell into the hands of the Nationalists when the war ended in March 1939.

The improved I-15bis was tested in early 1937 and was distinguished by a longer cowling (covering a more powerful engine), and streamlining spats on the undercarriage legs. Over 2400 examples had been built by the time production ceased in early 1939. By then it had also seen action against the Japanese in Manchuria. In the Winter War of 1939–40, the I-15bis was extensively used against the Finns. The few examples of the improved version that made it to fight in Spain were nicknamed "Super Chatos" by the Spanish.

In 1937–8, the I-15bis was sent in quantity, with pilots, to help Chinese Nationalists fight the Japanese who were invading. It was during these air battles that the tough biplane began to meet its match in some of the Japanese monoplanes. Nevertheless over 1000 I-15bis fighters were still in Soviet Air Force use in mid-1941 although most were used for ground attack. By late 1942 all were relegated to second-line duties.

Polikarpov I-15bis

First flight: October 1933 (prototype)
Power: M-25V 775hp radial piston engine
Armament: Four 7.62mm/0.3in machine-guns plus bombload of up to 150kg/331lb
Size: Wingspan – 10.2m/33ft 5.5in
Length – 6.27m/20ft 6.75in
Height – 2.19m/7ft 2.25in
Wing area – 22.53m^2/242.52sq ft
Weights: Empty – 1320kg/2910lb
Maximum take-off – 1900kg/4189lb
Performance: Maximum speed – 370kph/230mph
Ceiling – 9500m/31,170ft
Range – 530km/329 miles
Climb – 765m/2500ft per minute

Polikarpov I-16

LEFT: **The classic I-16 fighter was in the front line on at least four battle fronts.**

The tiny I-16, reminiscent of the American Gee Bee racing aircraft, was one of the most important and innovative fighters of its time. With a wooden fuselage, it was also the first widely used low-wing cantilever monoplane with retractable landing gear. It first flew in December 1933, and in the mid-1930s this aircraft was one of the world's best fighters – it had a good top speed some 123kph/70mph faster than its contemporaries, and was well-armed and highly manoeuvrable. It remained in production until 1939 by which time a host of variants had been developed.

It was not until the Spanish Civil War that the I-16 came to the attention of the Western world. The Republicans were supplied with 278 I-16s from October 1935. Hispano-Suiza also licence-built the I-16 for the Republicans in Spain but after their surrender, others were produced for the Franco régime. Many of the I-16s that saw action in Spain were flown by volunteer Soviet pilots.

In 1937, Soviet I-16s also saw service in China against the Japanese. From 1938 the Chinese flew the type and by 1939, Soviet I-16s were locked in fierce air battles with the Japanese on the Manchurian border.

The 1939–40 Winter War with Finland saw the Soviet I-16s in action again but by the time of the German invasion of Russia, the I-16 was seriously outclassed. Though suffering large losses, the I-16 fought on in the battles of 1941 with the often desperate heroism displayed by the Soviet pilots – some I-16s are known to have resorted to ramming enemy aircraft in attempts to stem the invasion. It was not until late 1943 that the I-16 was withdrawn from Soviet front-line service.

The I-16 was an excellent fighter for its time period, and fought on long after it should have been retired.

Polikarpov I-16 Type 24

First flight: December 31, 1933
Power: M-62 1000hp radial piston engine
Armament: Four 7.62mm/0.3in machine-guns – two in wings and two synchronized housed in forward fuselage
Size: Wingspan – 8.88m/29ft 1.5in
Length – 6.04m/19ft 9.75in
Height – 2.41m/7ft 10.75in
Wing area – 14.87m^2/160sq ft
Weights: Empty – 1475kg/3252lb
Maximum take-off – 2060kg/4542lb
Performance: Maximum speed – 490kph/304mph
Ceiling – 9470m/31,070ft
Range – 600km/373 miles
Climb – 850m/2790ft per minute

LEFT: **The Potez 63.11 variant was a tactical reconnaissance/ground version of the series.**

Potez 631

First flight: April 25, 1936 (Potez 630)
Power: Two Hispano-Suiza 725hp 14AB 14-cylinder two row radials
Armament: Two forward-firing 20mm/0.78in cannon and a flexibly mounted 7.5mm/0.3in machine-gun in the rear cockpit plus four 7.5mm/0.3in machine-guns mounted under the wings
Size: Wingspan – 16m/52ft 6in
Length – 11.07m/36ft 10.5in
Height – 3.04m/9ft 11.6in
Wing area – 32.7m²/351.99sq ft
Weights: Empty – 2838kg/6256lb
Maximum take-off – 3760kg/8289lb
Performance: Maximum speed – 442kph/275mph
Ceiling – 10,000m/32,800ft
Range – 1200km/758 miles
Climb – 4000m/13,125ft in 5 minutes, 56 seconds

Potez 630/631

The three-seat Potez 630 was built to a demanding French air ministry specification for a twin-engine strategic fighter and first flew in April 1936. It was for its time a thoroughly modern design, powered by slim engines and boasting the far from standard retractable undercarriage. The first production version was the 630, all 80 of which were grounded for a time due to a series of catastrophic engine failures. Their generally poor performance soon took them into second-line training duties. The 631 however, powered by Gnome-Rhône engines was a great success and over 200 were built for both the Armée de l'Air and the French Navy. During the Battle of France, 631s flying in both day- and nightfighter units accounted for 29 Luftwaffe aircraft. After the fall of France, surviving 631s were for a time operated by Vichy forces but were later seized and passed on to Romania as trainers and target tugs.

LEFT: **The P.Z.L. P.11 was no match for the Luftwaffe fighters it faced in the Blitzkrieg.**

P.Z.L. P.11c

First flight: August 1931
Power: P.Z.L./Bristol Mercury 645hp VI.S2 radial piston engine
Armament: Two 7.7mm/0.303in machine-guns plus light bombs carried beneath wings
Size: Wingspan – 10.72m/35ft 2in
Length – 7.55m/24ft 9.25in Height – 2.85m/9ft 4.25in Wing area – 17.9m²/192.68sq ft
Weights: Empty – 1147kg/2529lb
Maximum take-off – 1630kg/3594lb
Performance: Maximum speed – 390kph/242mph
Ceiling – 8000m/26,245ft
Range – 700km/435 miles
Climb – 800m/2625ft per minute

P.Z.L. P.11

As the Germans prepared to invade Poland in September 1939, the bulk of the poorly organized fighter force that faced them was made up of around 160 P.11s. These aircraft were derived from the Polish-designed P.6 and P.7 fighters that first flew in 1930. Pilot forward view from the cockpit of the P.7 was compromised by the large radial engine that powered it. Smaller diameter engines were tested to improve the view and this together with other refinements led to the P.11 that was produced in three differently engined versions. The major variant was the P.11c powered by Skoda or P.Z.L-built Bristol Mercury radials and deliveries to the Polish Air Force were complete by late 1936.

When the Germans launched their invasion of Poland, the P.11 pilots fought well and made the most of their outmoded machines. Some sources claim that 114 of the P.11s were destroyed in the air battles that raged at the time of the invasion – although the defence failed, the P.11s did destroy 126 Luftwaffe aircraft. A more heavily armed version of the P.11 was tested but finished aircraft did not reach the Polish fighter squadrons before the German invasion.

Reggiane Re.2000 fighters

TOP: **The US design influence is clear on this study of an early Re.2000.** ABOVE: **A few Re.2000s were exported to Sweden and Hungary; the latter nation also undertook its own production of the type.** LEFT: **Derivatives of the Re.2000 proved to be very potent fighter aircraft.**

Development of the Re.2000 began in 1937 and was clearly influenced by the chunky radial-engined fighters being developed in the USA at the time. When the Re.2000 Falco I prototype flew in 1938, the Italian Air Force appeared to show little interest, but the Italian Navy did order Serie II and Serie III versions for catapult launching and long-range missions respectively. The Hungarian Air Force also bought some Re.2000s and a few were manufactured in Hungary under licence – in Hungary the type was known as Hejja (hawk). Sweden also ordered 60 for the Swedish Air Force who operated the type until 1945.

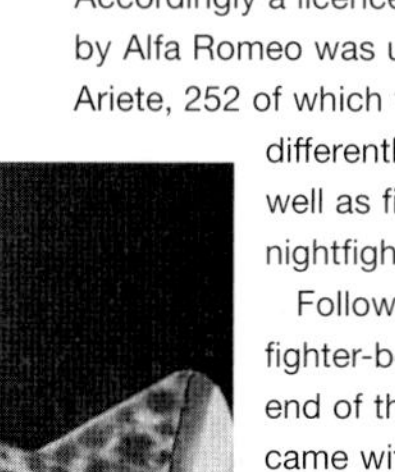

The German DB-601 in-line engine was trialled in a new version designated Re.2001 Ariete (ram) but Daimler-Benz had to focus on orders for the Luftwaffe. Accordingly a licence-built version made by Alfa Romeo was used to power the Ariete, 252 of which were built in three differently armed versions as well as fighter-bomber and nightfighter variants.

Following the Re.2002 fighter-bomber version, the end of the Re.2000 line came with the Re.2005 Sagittario which many consider to be the best Italian fighter of World War II. Powered by an in-line engine, the test flight took place in September 1942, and when it entered production it was powered by a licence-built DB 605. Although only 48 Sagittarios were built before the Allies overran the factories, these fighters were widely used to defend Naples, Rome and Sicily. As the Allies closed in on Berlin, a few fanatical pilots and their Re.2005s even fought on over the city.

Reggiane Re.2005 Sagittario

First flight: September 1942
Power: Fiat 1475hp RA.1050 RC.58 Tifone in-line piston engine
Armament: Three 20mm/0.78in cannon and two 12.7mm/0.5in machine-guns
Size: Wingspan – 11m/36ft 1in
Length – 8.73m/28ft 7.75in
Height – 3.15m/10ft 4in
Wing area – 20.4m²/219.59sq ft
Weights: Empty – 2600kg/5732lb
Maximum take-off – 3560kg/7848lb
Performance: Maximum speed – 630kph/391mph
Ceiling – 12,000m/39,370ft
Range – 1250km/777 miles
Climb – 1100m/3600ft per minute

Republic P-47 Thunderbolt

When the P-47 first flew in May 1941 it was the largest and heaviest single-seat piston fighter ever produced – it still is. Later versions, when fully loaded, weighed more than a loaded Luftwaffe Dornier Do 17 bomber. It was also produced in greater numbers than any other American fighter and was one of the outstanding US fighters of World War II.

Considerable technical difficulties were overcome in the development of the P-47 – making sure that the massive 3.7m/12ft-diameter propeller cleared the ground was a major concern, calling for very long landing gear which had to retract inwards to leave room for the heavy wing armament of eight 12.7mm/0.5in machine-guns. The deep fuselage was made to accommodate the large pipes and ducts that fed exhaust gas to the turbocharger in the rear fuselage or fed the high-pressure air back to the engine again. Among the cockpit innovations were cabin air-conditioning, variable gun-bay heating and electric fuel indicators.

The P-47B finally entered production in 1942 and Thunderbolts of the US Army Air Force began to arrive in Britain from early 1943 with the task of escorting Eighth Air Force B-17s and B-24s on hazardous daylight bombing raids over Europe. The first P-47 mission was in April 1943 and the "Jug" (short for juggernaut) excelled as a high-altitude escort fighter – in spite of its size it was agile and a favourite of pilots. P-47Cs introduced more powerful engines and provision for a belly tank – these auxiliary droppable fuel tanks were carried from March 1944, giving the Jugs the range to get them all the way to Berlin.

TOP: The mighty P-47 was a truly big aircraft – compare it to the slender Spitfire. ABOVE: This example, based at the Imperial War Museum Duxford in the UK, is a very popular participant in European air shows.

Thunderbolts were also formidable ground-attack aircraft and pilots were encouraged to indulge in train-busting for which the robustly constructed aircraft was ideally suited. It was a "get-you-home" aircraft that could absorb considerable damage. P-47s were also widely used by the UK-based US Ninth (tactical) Air Force, escorting their Havocs and Marauders.

The P-47D, produced from early 1943, was the definitive Thunderbolt and featured a host of improvements – a more powerful engine equipped for water injection emergency boost, a more efficient turbocharger, better pilot armour and multi-ply tyres to survive landings on the roughest of airstrips. The D model was also the first able to carry a 454kg/1000lb bomb under each wing as well as a belly tank – with three tanks the Jugs could go deep into enemy territory. Part way into D model production, the bubble canopy was introduced, replacing the old greenhouse type, and the removal of the "razorback" eradicated a blind spot to the rear. Unpainted aircraft were now also supplied from the factories, improving top speed slightly.

A special "hot-rod" version of the P-47D, the P-47M, was built in limited numbers and made its appearance in December 1944, to catch and destroy the V-1 flying bombs that Germany was launching against Allied targets. With a top speed of 756kph/470mph, the P-47M had airbrakes fitted to the wings so that it could decelerate once it had caught enemy aircraft. The P-47M certainly scored victories over German Me262 and Arado 234 jets.

ABOVE: **An early razorback version of the P-47 with the "greenhouse"-style canopy.** LEFT: **A P-47 of the 78th Fighter Group, US Eighth Air Force, in World War II.**

LEFT: **The Thunderbolt was equally at home in the low-level ground attack role.** ABOVE: **Preparing for another mission, these "razorbacks" are pictured just after D-Day.**

The long-range P-47N, the ultimate Thunderbolt, was virtually a complete redesign, with long-span wings containing fuel tanks. Produced from December 1944, it was intended for long-range operations in the Pacific and had square-tipped wings for better roll.

The Royal Air Force also used Thunderbolts from September 1944, but exclusively in the Far East against the Japanese. Sixteen RAF squadrons operated the type in both ground-attack and bomber escort missions but rarely had the opportunity to engage in a dogfight. Two RAF Thunderbolt squadrons continued in service in India until 1946 when the Tempest replaced it in Royal Air Force service.

By the end of World War II the P-47 had flown 546,000 missions and in Western Europe alone destroyed 3752 aircraft in air combat. The Jug was truly one of the greatest fighters ever and continued to equip air forces until the mid-1950s. A total of 15,660 P-47s were produced, of which 12,602 were D models.

Republic P-47D Thunderbolt

First flight: May 6, 1941 (XP-47B)
Power: Pratt & Whitney 2535hp R-2800-59 Double-Wasp eighteen-cylinder radial engine
Armament: Eight 12.7mm/0.5in machine-guns, plus provision for external load of bombs or rockets to maximum of 1134kg/2500lb
Size: Wingspan – 12.4m/40ft 9in
Length – 11.02m/36ft 1in Height – 4.47m/14ft8in
Wing area – 27.87m²/300sq ft
Weights: Empty – 4513kg/9950lb
Maximum take-off – 7938kg/17,500lb
Performance: Maximum speed – 697kph/433mph
Ceiling – 12,495m/41,000ft
Range – 3060km/1900 miles with three drop tanks
Climb – 976m/3200ft per minute

Royal Aircraft Factory S.E.5a

ABOVE: **The widely produced S.E.5a was a true classic fighter.** BELOW: **The air element of the American Expeditionary Force used the S.E.5a with great success.**

The robust and long-lived S.E.5a was one of the few World War I aircraft to enjoy a lengthy production run, with over 5000 produced in all, compared to, for example, the mere 150 Sopwith Triplanes that entered service. The S.E.5a was developed from the S.E.5, designed to make maximum use of a new Hispano-Suiza engine that appeared in 1915. The unarmed prototype, made almost entirely of wood with a fabric covering, first flew in November 1916. Two versions of the engine (150hp and 200hp) were proposed for the aircraft and although early examples had the 150hp powerplant, the 200hp version soon became the standard engine.

The S.E.5 first entered service with the Royal Flying Corps' No.56 Squadron, but its operational use in France was delayed until April 1917 as a factory-fitted wrap-around windscreen was found to obscure the pilot's forward vision and had to be removed from all machines. About 60 of the 150hp S.E.5s were built but they were gradually replaced on the production line and in the squadrons by the 200hp-engined S.E.5a. Other improvements incorporated in the S.E.5a were shorter wings resulting from the rear spar being shortened for greater strength and a headrest and fairing behind the cockpit to improve pilot comfort and streamlining.

The S.E.5a reached front-line squadrons in France in 1917 and was soon found to be capable of outfighting most enemy aircraft. But by December that year, only five RFC squadrons were equipped with the S.E.5a, production delays being caused by the continued slow delivery of engines – literally hundreds of aircraft sat engineless. But when the S.E.5a finally reached the front line in quantity, the very capable fighter served extensively over the Western Front with British, Australian and American pilots of the US American Expeditionary Force. They were also deployed in

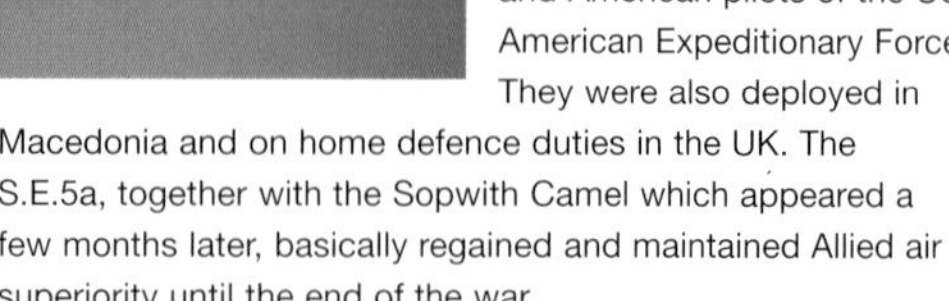

Macedonia and on home defence duties in the UK. The S.E.5a, together with the Sopwith Camel which appeared a few months later, basically regained and maintained Allied air superiority until the end of the war.

The S.E.5a became the favoured mount of some of World War I's most successful Allied fighter pilots, including British flying ace Albert Ball, who initially described the S.E.5 as a "bloody awful machine". Other S.E.5 aces included Longton, Clayson, Shields, Maxwell, Mannock and McCudden.

LEFT: **Some of the Allies' highest scoring pilots owed their success to the performance of the S.E.5a.**

BELOW: **Victoria Cross recipient Captain Albert Ball pictured in the cockpit of a No.56 Squadron S.E.5a.**

By the time the war ended, 22 RFC and US Air Service units were flying the S.E.5a. Over 5000 had been built in just under 18 months by five companies – Austin, Bleriot & SPAD, Martinsyde, Vickers and Wolseley.

After World War I, hundreds of these fighters were passed on to air forces throughout the British Empire. The American Expeditionary Force had bought 38 S.E.5as in Britain during the war and the design was selected for US production. Wartime plans to licence-build 1000 examples of the S.E.5a in the USA for the US Air Service were scrapped after the Armistice. Only one Curtiss S.E.5a was completed in the USA but 56 more were completed in the 1922–3 period from components shipped from Britain. These were later converted for use as advanced trainers in the USA.

LEFT: **Members of No.1 Squadron RAF and their S.E.5as pictured on July 3, 1918.**

After the end of World War I the fighter was dropped from military inventories and hundreds were sold on to civilian operators. In 1921, one example went to Japan with the British aviation mission and is considered to have greatly influenced later single-seat fighter design in Japan. S.E.5as were also widely used to pioneer the advertising phenomenon of skywriting, spelling out company names in the air using trails of smoke.

ABOVE: **As well as their use on the Western Front, S.E.5as were also used defending Britain on home defence duties.**

Royal Aircraft Factory S.E.5a

First flight: November 22, 1916 (S.E.5)

Power: Wolseley 200hp Viper V-8 water-cooled engine

Armament: One synchronized 7.7mm/0.303in machine-gun, mounted off-centre on top of engine, plus another on a flexible mount in front of cockpit. Four 11.3kg/25lb bombs could be carried under the fuselage

Size: Wingspan – 8.12m/26ft 7.5in
Length – 6.38m/20ft 11in Height – 2.9m/9ft 6in
Wing area – 22.67m²/44sq ft

Weights: Empty – 649kg/1430lb
Maximum take-off – 880kg/1940lb

Performance: Maximum speed – 222kph/138mph
Ceiling – 5180m/17,000ft
Range – 2.5 hours endurance
Climb – 3050m/10,000ft in 13.25 minutes

Royal Aircraft Factory F.E. series

The Royal Aircraft Factory first started building the F.E.2 (F.E. stood for Fighter Experimental) in 1913. The F.E.2 was what was known as a pusher aircraft, that is the propeller was used to push from behind rather than pull from the front as in tractor aircraft.

The pusher arrangement was born, in the days before the invention of interrupter gear, of the need for a forward-firing gun

and the removal of the propeller, which tended to get in the way of the bullets. With no propeller in the way, the front seat was given to the gunner/observer while the pilot occupied the rear seat. Disadvantages of the pusher arrangement included the danger of anything flying out of the aircraft hitting the propeller, sometimes damaging or destroying it. Although the engine could protect the pilot if attacked from behind, in the event of a nose-down crash the engine and associated fuel tended to land on top of the two-man crew.

Early Fees, as they were known, had a 100hp engine which was soon replaced in the F.E.2b by a 120hp Beardmore engine. This was itself later supplanted by 160hp Beardmores which improved the aircraft's top speed and performance. The ultimate development of the Fee was the F.E.2d powered by a 250hp Rolls-Royce engine.

In combat the F.E.2b, along with the Airco D.H.2, kept the Fokkers at bay and it was an F.E.2b that shot down the German ace Max Immelmann in June 1916. This version was however soon outclassed by the latest German Albatros and Halberstadt fighting scouts so the F.E.2d was brought to the Front in 1916. F.E.2bs did however serve until the end of the war on UK home defence against Zeppelins and Gotha bombers.

ABOVE: **This F.E.2b, serial A5666, is shown minus the usual nosewheel installation.** LEFT: **A rare air-to-air shot of a "Fee" in its element.** BELOW: **An F.E.2d of No.20 Squadron, Royal Flying Corps, pictured in 1916.**

Royal Aircraft Factory F.E.2b

First flight: August 1913 (F.E.)
Power: Beardmore 120hp in-line piston engine
Armament: Up to two 7.7mm/0.303in machine-guns
Size: Wingspan – 14.55m/47ft 9in
Length – 9.83m/32ft 3in
Height – 3.85m/12ft 7.5in
Wing area – 45.89m²/494sq ft
Weights: Empty – 904kg/1993lb
Maximum take-off – 1347kg/2970lb
Performance: Maximum speed – 129kph/80mph
Ceiling – 2745m/9000ft
Range – 3 hours endurance
Climb – 3050m/10,000ft in 51 minutes, 45 seconds

The single-seat F.E.8 pusher biplane was developed again because of the lack of an effective British interrupter gear and entered service on the Western Front in August 1916. Although lighter and more manoeuvrable than the F.E.2, the F.E.8 was no better a fighter as the pilot had to deal with the machine-gun (which was prone to stoppages) while still flying the aircraft and looking for the enemy. Nine F.E.8s were effectively destroyed in a single engagement with a formation led by Baron von Richthofen and by mid-1917 all F.E.8s were withdrawn from front-line use.

Royal Aircraft Factory F.E.8

First flight: October 15, 1915
Power: Gnome Monosoupape 100hp rotary piston engine
Armament: One 7.7mm/0.303in machine-guns
Size: Wingspan – 9.6m/31ft 6in
Length – 7.21m/23ft 8in
Height – 2.79m/9ft 2in
Wing area – 20.25m²/218sq ft
Weights: Empty – 406kg/895lb
Maximum take-off – 610kg/1345lb
Performance: Maximum speed – 151kph/94mph
Ceiling – 4420m/14,500ft
Range – 2 hours, 30 minutes endurance
Climb – 1830m/6000ft in 9 minutes, 28 seconds

Siemens-Schuckert D-series fighters

Throughout the history of aviation, good designs have both inspired competitors and been copied by enemies. The Siemens-Schuckert D-series of fighters began in 1916 with the D I that was an improved copy of the Nieuport XI. The arrival of the French fighter was a severe problem for Germany and, as no better aircraft was in the German design pipeline, they decided to copy it instead. Three German companies were ordered to produce improved copies of the Nieuport, and Siemens-Schuckert did the best job. Powered by a 110hp rotary engine and armed with one synchronized 7.9mm/0.31in machine-gun, the D I was otherwise identical to the French aircraft. During early tests in October 1916, the aircraft made an impressive climb to 5000m/16,405ft in 45 minutes. Although 150 aircraft were ordered, engine production problems delayed their delivery and by mid-1917 only 95 had been completed. By then other aircraft with better performance were available and so, when the D I finally made it to the Western Front, it was used mainly for training.

The Siemens-Schuckert D III with its circular section fuselage was built around the new 160hp Siemens-Halske Sh III rotary engine. The D III was derived from D II prototypes that first flew in June 1917. Just like the D I, engine development had delayed the D II programme and unreliability was initially a problem on the D III. However, when the engine's teething problems were resolved, the D III proved to have great potential as an interceptor due its good rate of climb. Unfortunately its level speed was not high enough for it to be a viable modern fighter, so the type was used to trial aerodynamic refinements which led to the D IV fighter version. The D IV had the same impressive climb as the D III and all-round performance was improved. The first of around 60 D IVs to see service reached front-line units in August 1918 but it was a case of too little too late to make a difference. Strangely, production of the D IV was allowed to continue after the Armistice until mid-1919.

ABOVE: **With its origins in a Nieuport XI copy, the D-series evolved into some worthwhile fighter types.**
LEFT: **A number of D-Series replicas fly in the USA.**

Siemens-Schuckert D III

First flight: October 1917
Power: Siemens-Halske 160hp Sh III rotary piston engine
Armament: Two fixed forward-firing 7.92mm/0.31in machine-guns
Size: Wingspan – 8.43m/27ft 7.75in
Length – 5.7m/18ft 8.5in
Height – 2.8m/9ft 2.25in
Wing area – 18.9m²/203.44sq ft
Weights: Empty – 534kg/1177lb
Maximum take-off – 725kg/1598lb
Performance: Maximum speed – 180kph/112mph
Ceiling – 8000m/26,245ft
Range – 2 hours endurance
Climb – 5000m/16,400ft in 13 minutes

TOP AND ABOVE: **Though replicas, these two aircraft salute World War I's most effective fighter aircraft, the Sopwith Camel.**

Sopwith Camel

The Camel, arguably the best-known aircraft of the World War I period, is now credited with the destruction of around 3000 enemy aircraft, making it by far the most effective fighter of the War. It evolved from the Sopwith Pup (which it replaced in service) and Triplane but was much more of a handful than its Sopwith stablemates. It was extremely sensitive on the controls and its forward-placed centre of gravity (due to the concentration of the engine, armament, pilot and fuel in the front 2.17m/7ft of the fuselage) made it very easy to turn. It earned a reputation for weeding out the less able student pilots in the most final of ways but in skilled hands the Camel was an excellent fighter and virtually unbeatable. Like the Pup, the Sopwith Biplane F.1 became better known by its nickname, in this case the Camel, and the official designation is largely forgotten.

The prototype, powered by a 110hp Clerget 9Z engine, first flew at Brooklands in February 1917 and was followed by the F.1/3 pre-production model. First deliveries were to the RNAS No.4 (Naval) Squadron at Dunkirk, who received their new fighter in June 1917. The first Camel air victory occurred on June 4, when Flight Commander A.M. Shook sent a German aircraft down into the sea – on the next day Shook attacked 15 enemy aircraft and probably destroyed two of them. The RFC's first Camel victory was achieved by Captain C. Collett on June 27.

One manoeuvre unique to the Camel was an incredibly quick starboard turn, assisted by the torque of the big rotary engine. So fast was the right turn that pilots were able to use it to great advantage in combat, sometimes choosing to make three-quarter right turns in place of the slower quarter turn to the left. It was risky, however, as during the sharp right turns, the nose tried to go violently downwards and a left turn brought a tendency to climb, all due to the torque of the engine. Camels were built equipped with a variety of engines, including the Clerget 9B, Bentley BR1, Gnome Monosoupape and Le Rhône 9J.

In the Battle of Cambrai in March 1918, Captain J.L. Trollope of No.43 Squadron used his Camel to shoot down six enemy aircraft in one day, March 24. Later that year Camels were in the thick of what many historians believe to be the greatest dogfight of World War I. On the morning of November 4, 1918 Camels of Nos.65 and 204 Squadrons attacked 40 Fokker D. VIIs. The pilots of No.65 claimed eight

LEFT: **One of the very early Sopwith-built Camel F.1s, serial N6332.** ABOVE: **Major William Barker V.C., D.S.O., M.C., at one time commander of No.28 Squadron, with his personal Camel.**

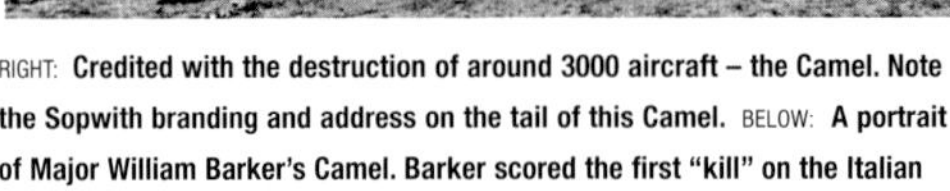

RIGHT: **Credited with the destruction of around 3000 aircraft – the Camel. Note the Sopwith branding and address on the tail of this Camel.** BELOW: **A portrait of Major William Barker's Camel. Barker scored the first "kill" on the Italian Front, flying in the famous Sopwith fighter.**

destroyed, six out of control and one driven down while the pilots of 204 claimed two destroyed and five out of control. Perhaps the most famous single Camel victory is, however, that of Canadian Camel pilot Roy Brown, who was credited with the death of Manfred von Richthofen, the "Red Baron", on April 21, 1918.

Camels were also operated against the Austro-Hungarians on the Italian Front, and Major William Barker scored the first British victory in that theatre while flying a Camel on November 29, 1917.

By the end of 1917 over 1000 Camels were delivered and work began on sub-variants. Camels that went to sea on the early aircraft carriers had a removable tail for easy stowage. Those specially designed for shipboard use were designated 2F.1 Camel and were the last type of Camel built. Many stayed in use after the war. A ground-attack version with downward-firing Lewis guns was developed – called the TF.1 (trench fighter), it did not go into production.

Nightfighter Camels on home defence duties in the UK were powered by the Le Rhône engine and were armed with two Lewis guns above the upper wing, in place of the usual twin-Vickers that fired through the propeller arc. They were widely used against the German Gotha bombers. As part of experiments to provide British airships with their own fighter defence, Camels were experimentally launched from a cradle beneath airship R.23.

In addition to the RFC, RNAS and RAF, Camels were also operated by Belgium, Canada, Greece and the air element of the American Expeditionary Force. The Slavo-British Aviation Group also operated Camels in Russia in 1918. Total Camel production was around 5500.

Sopwith F.1 Camel

First flight: February 26, 1917
Power: Clerget 130hp 9-cylinder air-cooled rotary piston engine
Armament: Two 7.7mm/0.303in synchronized Vickers machine-guns on nose, plus four 11.35kg/25lb bombs carried below fuselage
Size: Wingspan – 8.53m/28ft
Length – 5.72m/18ft 9in
Height – 2.6m/8ft 6in
Wing area – 21.46m²/231sq ft
Weights: Empty – 421kg/929lb
Maximum take-off – 659kg/1453lb
Performance: Maximum speed – 188kph/117mph
Ceiling – 5790m/19,000ft
Range – 2 hours, 30 minutes endurance
Climb – 3050m/10,000ft in 10 minutes, 35 seconds

LEFT: **The well-armed Sopwith Dolphin.**

Sopwith 5F.1 Dolphin

First flight: May 22, 1917
Power: Hispano-Suiza 200hp piston engine
Armament: Two forward-firing synchronized 7.7mm/0.303in machine-guns plus one or two machine-guns mounted in front of the cockpit, fixed to fire obliquely forward
Size: Wingspan – 9.91m/32ft 6in
Length – 6.78m/22ft 3in Height – 2.59m/8ft 6in
Wing area – 24.46m^2/263sq ft
Weights: Empty – 671kg/1480lb
Maximum take-off – 911kg/2008lb
Performance: Maximum speed – 180kph/112mph
Ceiling – 6095m/20,000ft
Range – 315km/195 miles
Climb – 260m/855ft per minute

Sopwith Dolphin

By the time the Dolphin first flew in May 1917, Sopwith had produced an impressive line of fighting aircraft, each benefiting from the experiences gained producing earlier models. With the Dolphin, prime design considerations were armament and pilot view from the cockpit. The pilot's all-round view was indeed excellent as his head poked through a gap in the centre section of the top wing which was mounted very close to the deep section fuselage.

The Dolphin Mk I entered service in 1917 and of the 1532 Dolphins produced a small number were also Mk II and Mk IIIs powered by different engines.

Dolphins were apparently not very popular with some pilots – their protruding head was vulnerable in nose-over landing incidents and the unusual back-staggered wing created odd stalling characteristics. Pilots' concerns for their safety led to the addition of a crash pylon above the top wing centre section, to prevent the aircraft slamming on to the top wing. Some pilots ran up impressive tallies of victories in Dolphins, including a Captain Gillett of No.79 Squadron who destroyed 14 enemy aircraft and three balloons.

LEFT: **The Pup was an excellent dogfighter.**

Sopwith Pup

First flight: February 1916
Power: Le Rhône 80hp rotary engine
Armament: One forward-firing synchronized Vickers 7.7mm/0.303 machine-gun, plus up to four 11.3kg/25lb bombs on external racks
Size: Wingspan – 8.08m/26ft 6in
Length – 6.04m/19ft 3.75in Height – 2.87m/9ft 5in
Wing area – 23.6m^2/254sq ft
Weights: Empty – 357kg/787 lb
Maximum take-off – 556kg/1225 lb
Performance: Maximum speed – 180kph/112mph
Ceiling – 5335m/17,500ft
Range – 3 hours endurance
Climb – 4911m/16,100ft in 35 minutes

Sopwith Pup

The Pup was the Allies' best answer to the Fokker Scourge and from late 1916 helped them turn the tide on the Western Front. Originally known as the Admiralty Type 9901, it retained the interplane struts (between the upper and lower wing) used on the Sopwith 1½-Strutter, but as its wings were 20 per cent smaller, the nickname of "Pup" was given and eventually kept as the official name. The Pup was manoeuvrable and a fine dogfighter. It entered Royal Naval Air Service (RNAS) and Royal Flying Corps service in 1916, soon earning a reputation as a formidable foe. It was responsive even at high altitude, and fully aerobatic up to 4575m/15,000ft. No.8 (Naval) Squadron accounted for 20 enemy aircraft with the Pup within little over two months in late 1916.

Production of this potent fighter exceeded 1770. Examples powered by the 100hp Gnome Monosoupape rotary engine were used for home defence in Britain, the larger engine markedly improving the Pup's performance.

RNAS Pups were used to pioneer the use of aircraft from Royal Navy ships – one flown on August 2, 1917 became the first aircraft to land on a ship underway.

Sopwith Snipe

The Sopwith Snipe was the last significant aircraft produced by Thomas Sopwith during World War I. Designed and developed by Herbert Smith in late 1917, the Snipe was an improved version of the Sopwith Camel with a new engine, the 230hp Bentley rotary, which enabled it to fly faster and higher than its predecessor.

The Snipe was, by 1918, considered to be the best Allied fighter plane on the Western Front and was praised by pilots for its speed, strength and agility. The view from the cockpit was much better than that of the Camel which was particularly important on nightflying. Almost 500 Snipes were built in 1918 and eventually 1567 were delivered to the Royal Air Force.

The Snipe introduced a number of innovations including electric cockpit heating and pilot oxygen. Although the Snipe reached the front line only eight weeks before the end of the war, its few encounters with the enemy showed its clear superiority. On October 27, 1918 Major William Barker, in a Snipe of No.201 Squadron RAF, came upon no fewer than 60 Fokker D. VIIs, 15 of which attacked him repeatedly. He took them all on single-handed, destroyed four and probably two others before he crash-landed his bullet-ridden Snipe weak from loss of blood from wounds sustained in his epic aerial battle against seemingly overwhelming odds. Barker was awarded the Victoria Cross for his action.

LEFT: **This largely forgotten British fighter protected the UK for a number of years after the end of World War I.** BELOW: **For a time the best British fighter available, over 1500 examples of the Sopwith Snipe reached RAF squadrons.**

Sopwith Snipe

First flight: September 1917
Power: Bentley 230hp B.R.2 rotary piston engine
Armament: Two forward-firing synchronized 7.7mm/0.303in machine-guns
Size: Wingspan – 9.17m/30ft 1in
Length – 6.02m/19ft 9in
Height – 2.67m/8ft 9in
Wing area – 25.08m^2/270sq ft
Weights: Empty – 595kg/1312lb
Maximum take-off – 916kg/2020lb
Performance: Maximum speed – 195kph/121mph
Ceiling – 5945m/19,500ft
Range – 3 hours endurance
Climb – 460m/1500ft per minute

After the war the Snipe remained the most important fighter in the RAF, and up until 1923 it constituted Britain's only fighter defence, remaining in service until 1927.

TOP: **In a climb, no contemporary fighter could match the performance of the "Tripehound".** ABOVE: **The Royal Naval Air Service was a very effective user of the Triplane.** LEFT: **The Triplane was so impressive in action that the Germans were desperate to develop their own equivalent, which resulted in the Fokker Dr.I Triplane.**

Sopwith Triplane

Following the success of the Sopwith Pup, the Sopwith Triplane was designed and built in 1916 and combined what were thought at the time to be the prime performance requirements for a fighter – high rate of climb and excellent manoeuvrability. In what was

really a daring experiment the new aircraft was built using a fuselage and tail unit similar to that of the Sopwith Pup, a more powerful engine and the all-important extra wing. Although it could not outmanoeuvre the earlier Pup, the Triplane could outclimb any other aircraft, friendly and hostile.

After its first flight in May 1916, the prototype was sent to France immediately for combat trials and became the first triplane fighter on the Western Front. Within only 15 minutes of its arrival in France, it was sent up to attack a German aircraft. Observers were amazed at the Triplane's ability to get to 3660m/12,000ft in only 13 minutes.

The enthusiastic response of its first pilots got the Sopwith rushed into production for service with the Royal Naval Air Service, who flew it with devastating effect between February and July 1917. The all-Canadian "B" Flight (nicknamed "Black Flight") of No.10 Squadron RNAS alone notched up 87 kills in Triplanes in less than 12 weeks. German pilots actively avoided flights of Triplanes. Such was the impact of the Tripehound, as the Sopwith came to be affectionately known, that the German High Command offered a substantial prize for an aircraft of equal capability. Anthony Fokker had set about designing his own triplane before a captured example could be examined. It is hard to believe that this small fighter, of which only 140 examples were built, had the upper hand over enemy fighters for so long.

Sopwith Triplane

First flight: May 28, 1916
Power: Clerget 130hp rotary piston engine
Armament: One or two forward-firing synchronized 7.7mm/0.303in Vickers machine-guns
Size: Wingspan – 8.08m/26ft 6in
Length – 5.74m/18ft 10in Height – 3.2m/10ft 6in
Wing area – 21.46m^2/231sq ft
Weights: Empty – 499kg/1101lb
Maximum take-off – 699kg/1541lb
Performance: Maximum speed – 188kph/117mph
Ceiling – 6250m/20,500ft
Range – 2 hours, 45 minutes
Climb – 366m/1200ft per minute

SPAD S.XIII

First flight: April 4, 1917
Power: Hispano-Suiza 220hp 8Be piston engine
Armament: Two forward-firing synchronized 7.7mm/0.303 machine-guns
Size: Wingspan – 8.1m/26ft 6.75in
Length – 6.3m/20ft 8in
Height – 2.35m/7ft 8.5in
Wing area – 20.2m^2/217.44sq ft
Weights: Empty – 601kg/1326lb
Maximum take-off – 845kg/1863lb
Performance: Maximum speed – 215kph/134mph
Ceiling – 6650m/21,815ft
Range – 2 hours endurance
Climb – 2000m/6560ft in 4 minutes, 40 seconds

SPAD S. series fighters

The SPAD (Société Pour l'Aviation et ses Dérivés) S.VII, the French company's first really successful military aircraft, took to the air for the first time in April 1916. It showed such promise that it was put into production immediately. The S.VII was an immediate success, mainly because of its sturdy construction, which permitted it to dive at high speeds without disintegrating. Two engine types were used to power the S.VII – the 150hp Hispano-Suiza 8Aa and the 180hp 8Ac.

By September 1916 it began to appear at the Front in both French and British (Royal Flying Corps and Royal Naval Air Service) fighter squadrons. The sought-after fighter was also operated by the Belgians, the Italians and the Russians. The famed Escadrille Lafayette, made up of American pilots, was operating the SPAD VII in February 1918 at the time it transferred from the French forces to the Air Service of the American Expeditionary Force (AEF) and became the 103rd Aero Squadron. More than 6,000 SPAD S.VIIs were built, of which 189 were purchased by the AEF.

The success of the S.VII inevitably led to developments of the aircraft, such as the S.XIII, designed in 1916 to counter the twin-gun German fighters. It had an increased wingspan and a more powerful engine, plus other aerodynamic refinements. The highly successful S.XIII doubled the firepower of the earlier S.VII by mounting two 7.7mm/0.303in machine-guns. French test pilots enthused about the aircraft and the French government ordered more than 2000 – in the end almost 8500 were built. It began to enter service with French units on the Western Front late in May 1917, replacing S.VIIs and Nieuports, and became the mount of the French aces Nungesser, Fonck and Guynemer.

The Royal Flying Corps operated the S.XIII as did the air forces of Italy and Belgium. The US Air Service also began operating the S.XIII in March 1918, and by the end of the war in November 1918 it had acquired 893. Throughout 1917 and into 1918 the S.XIII held its own against German aircraft, but during the summer of 1918 it was outclassed by the new Fokker D. VII. Nevertheless, at the war's end, outstanding orders for more than 10,000 examples were cancelled, such had been the demand for this excellent fighter aircraft.

TOP LEFT: **The French "Cicognes" Group de Chasse 12 were famed for the flying stork insignia carried on their aircraft.** ABOVE: **The SPAD S.XIII, a replica in this example, was a great fighter aircraft.** BELOW: **Another distinctive scheme, the famous "hat in the hoop" insignia on this replica SPAD S. XIII was sported by aircraft of the 94th Squadron, US Air Service. This aircraft is painted as the personal aircraft of American ace Eddie Rickenbacker.**

Supermarine Spitfire

The Spitfire is perhaps the most famous combat aircraft of all time, and some would say the most beautiful. Spitfires first entered Royal Air Force service at RAF Duxford in August 1938 and it was on October 16, 1939 that a Spitfire of No.603 Squadron claimed the first German aircraft, a Heinkel He111, to be destroyed over Britain in World War II.

The Spitfire Mk I is the model inevitably associated with Britain's Finest Hour, but by the time the Mk Is were battling to keep the Germans from invading Britain, the Spitfire had undergone a series of modifications that made it quite different to the aircraft that first entered RAF service in 1938. At the start of the Battle of Britain, Fighter Command could field a total of 19 Spitfire squadrons. Although some Mk IIs reached squadron service during the battle, it is the Mk I Spitfire that will forever be considered the Spitfire that won the Battle of Britain. During 1941 the Spitfire Mk I was relegated from the front line but its work was done – the Spitfire had earned a special place in the nation's heart and it had already become a legend.

The Spitfire Mk V began to reach RAF squadrons in February 1941 and swiftly became Fighter Command's primary weapon. Six thousand Mk Vs entered service between 1941 and 1943 and the type equipped more than 140 RAF squadrons, as well as nine overseas air forces, including the USAAF in Europe. Throughout 1941 the Mk V took part in fighter sweeps over occupied Europe, its range boosted by drop tanks. In 1942

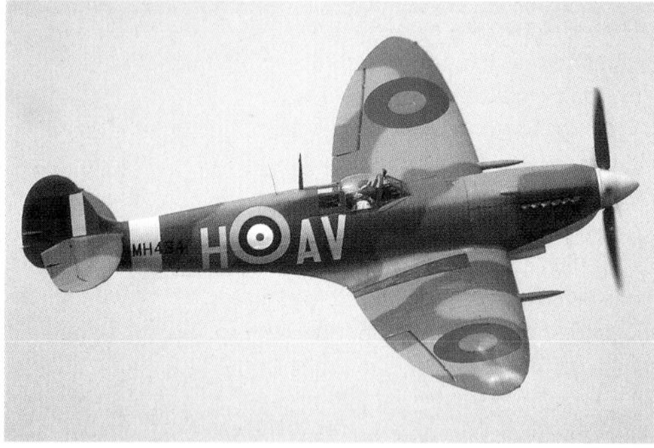

TOP: R.J. Mitchell's classic design, the Supermarine Spitfire, is surely the most famous of all fighters and has earned itself a special place in history, not just for what it achieved but also for what it represented. ABOVE: This Mk IX, MH434, is operated in the UK by the Old Flying Machine Company and has delighted crowds at air shows for decades.

Mk Vs were used in support of the Dieppe landings, fought in the North African campaign, defended Malta, took part in Operation Torch and were supplied to the USSR. In 1943 they even moved as far afield as Australia to defend against attack by Japanese aircraft.

When the Spitfire Mk IX was introduced in June 1942, it offered the RAF a much-needed counter to the deadly Focke-Wulf 190. With its armament of two 20mm/0.788in cannon, four .303 machine-guns and up to 2540kg/1000lb of bombs or rockets, the Spitfire Mk IX was indeed a potent fighting machine.

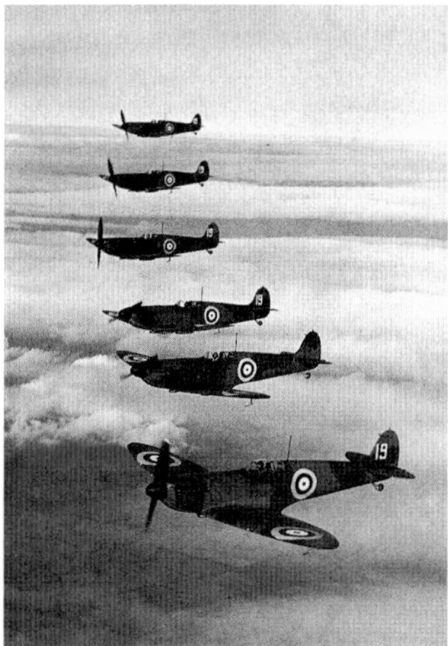

ABOVE: **The first of many – these early No.19 Squadron machines are shown with two blade propellers and unusual pre-war squadron numbers painted on the tails.** BELOW: **MB882, a late production Mk XII, in classic pose. Note the clipped wings, changing the distinctive "Spit" wing shape for better handling at low altitude.**

ABOVE: **This Mk V, preserved in the UK by the Shuttleworth Collection, was operated by No.310 (Czechoslovakian) Squadron during World War II and is seen in its wartime scheme.** LEFT: **An excellent wartime photograph of a Spitfire preparing to depart for another sortie.**

The Mk IX went on to equip around 100 RAF and Commonwealth fighter squadrons and later had the distinction of destroying several Me262 jets.

Designed to operate at high altitude, the Spitfire Mk XIV entered RAF service in January 1944 with 610 (City of Chester) Squadron. With a top speed of almost 724kph/450mph, it was capable of catching and destroying the V-1 flying bombs that were then menacing Britain. By the end of the war, the Mk XIV had accounted for more than 300 "doodlebugs". Compared to the early Merlin-engined Spitfire, the Mk XIV with its new fin and larger rudder was almost 1m/3ft longer and weighed up to 1224kg/2700lb more. In October 1944 a Mk XIV claimed a Messerschmitt Me262 jet fighter, the first to be shot down by an Allied aircraft, and in December of that year RAF Spitfire Mk XIVs carried out the heaviest fighter-bomber attack of World War II on V-2 rocket sites. A total of 957 Spitfire Mk XIVs were built, and the later Mk XVIII was directly developed from this powerful fighting machine.

Post-war, the Spitfire was widely used by many air forces but the last operational sortie of an RAF Spitfire was by a PR.19 of No.81 Squadron in Malaya on April 1, 1954. In all, over 20,000 Spitfires and Seafires (the naval version) were built by the time production ceased in 1949.

Supermarine Spitfire Mk Va

First flight: March 5, 1936
Power: Rolls-Royce 1478hp Merlin 45 liquid cooled V-12 engine
Armament: Eight 7.7m/0.303in machine-guns
Size: Wingspan – 11.23m/36ft 10in
Length – 9.12m/29ft 11in
Height – 3.02m/9ft 11in
Wing area – 22.48m²/242sq ft
Weights: Empty – 2267kg/4998lb
Maximum take-off – 2911kg/6417lb
Performance: Maximum speed – 594kph/369mph
Ceiling – 11,125m/36,500ft
Range – 1827km/1135 miles
Climb – 6100m/20,000ft in 7 minutes, 30 seconds

TOP: **The distinctive gull-wing of the Corsair is evident in this photograph of a preserved example.** ABOVE: **Initial US Navy reservations led to the type being considered unsuitable for operation from US carriers.**

Vought F4U Corsair

The Corsair was undoubtedly one of the greatest ever fighters. Designers Igor Sikorsky and Rex Beisel employed the largest propeller and most powerful engine ever fitted to a fighter aircraft, the latter a 2000hp Pratt and Whitney R-2800 Double Wasp. It was no surprise when, in 1940, the prototype Corsair exceeded 640kph/400mph, the first American combat aircraft to do so. It was equipped with a variety of armament over its long career but the Corsair was originally designed to carry two wing and two fuselage guns. Six 12.7mm/0.5in Browning machine-guns became standard, carried in the outer section of the foldable wings. Cannon and rockets were later added to the weapon options.

Ironically, as one of the fastest and most powerful fighters of World War II, the Corsair was originally rejected by the US Navy, who considered it unsuitable for carrier operations. Poor cockpit visibility and a tendency to bounce on landing meant that when, in February 1943 over Guadalcanal, the US Marines got the first chance to use the formidable fighter in action, it was as a land-based rather than carrier-based aircraft. It swiftly established itself as an excellent combat aircraft and the first Allied fighter able to take on the Japanese Zero on equal terms. The Corps was so impressed by the Corsair that all Marine squadrons re-equipped with the type within six months of its début. Marine Corsair pilot Major Gregory "Pappy" Boyington became the Corps' highest scoring pilot, ending the war with a total of 28 victories.

By the end of the year the mighty bent-wing fighter, operating purely from land, had accounted for over 500 Japanese aircraft. It was nicknamed "Whistling Death" by Japanese troops, who came to fear the noise made by air rushing through the diving Corsair's cooler vents heralding a deadly attack. By the end of World War II, the Corsair's total tally had increased to 2140 enemy aircraft destroyed in air combat, with over 64,000 air combat and ground attack missions recorded.

The Corsair's first use as a carrier fighter was with Britain's Fleet Air Arm, who had each of the aircraft's distinctive gull-wings clipped by around 20cm/8in to allow its stowage in the below-deck hangars on Royal Navy carriers. This début, in April 1944, was an attack on the German battleship *Tirpitz*. The Corsair became the principal aircraft of the FAA in the Pacific and almost 2000 were supplied to the Royal Navy and the Royal New Zealand Air Force.

"In dogfights the Corsair could out-turn most contemporary aircraft and in a dive, she could out-run anything," said Keith Quilter, FAA Corsair pilot.

The Corsair's outstanding performance led to extensive post-war use, notably in Korea, where they flew 80 per cent of all US Navy and Marine close-support missions in the conflict's first year, 1950. Nightfighter versions were particularly successful during the conflict, and during daytime combats the Corsairs even engaged and destroyed MiG-15s.

When production ceased in 1952, over 12,500 had been built, giving the Corsair one of the longest US fighter production runs in history. The late F2G version was powered by the 3000hp Pratt and Whitney R-4350 Wasp Major engine, which was 50 per cent more powerful than the Corsair's original powerplant.

The Corsair continued to serve in the front line for a number of years, and French naval pilots operated Corsairs from land bases during the anti-guerrilla war against the Viet Minh in Indochina from 1952 to 1954.

The Corsair was built in a number of versions, from the F4U-1 to the F4U-7. The designation differed when aircraft were produced by other manufacturers – Brewster (F3A) and Goodyear (FG, F2G).

TOP: **The Corsair's designers utilized the most powerful engine available.** LEFT: **Fleet Air Arm Corsairs first went into action in April 1944.**

BELOW: **The space-saving effect of wing folding and the location of the six wing-mounted guns can be seen in this photograph.**

ABOVE: **Royal Navy versions of the Vought fighter had to be slightly clipped for Fleet Air Arm carrier use.**

Vought F4U Corsair

First flight: May 29, 1940
Power: Pratt and Whitney 2000 hp R-2800-8 18-cylinder Double Wasp two-row air-cooled radial engine
Armament: Six 12.7mm/0.5in machine-guns with total of 2350 rounds – C model had four M2 cannon
Size: Wingspan – 12.5 m/41ft
Length – 10.15m/33ft 4in
Height – 4.9m/16ft 1in
Wing area – 29.17 m^2/314sq ft
Weights: Empty – 4074kg/8982lb
Loaded – 6350kg/14,000lb
Performance: Maximum speed – 671kph/417mph
Ceiling – 11,247m/36,900ft
Range – 1633km/1015 miles
Climb – 951m/3120ft per minute

Yakovlev wartime fighters

The Ya-26 fighter, made mostly of wood, was first flown in March 1939, having been designed to meet a Soviet requirement for a standard Soviet fighter. When it entered production it was as the I-26 but it was then redesignated the Yak-1. Production had barely begun when Germany invaded in June 1941. Designed to be as simple to manufacture as possible, the Yak was surprisingly agile and fast for its time. The Yak-1 had considerably closed the fighter gap that existed at the beginning of Russo-German hostilities and was able to hold its own to some degree with the Bf109. Total production was 8721.

Development was ongoing and the Yak-3 was a further development of a Yak-1 variant now referred to as the Yak-1M. First flown in late 1943, the Yak-3 proved to be an extremely capable dogfighter with outstanding manoeuvrability and a very high rate of climb. When it reached operational units in July 1944, the Luftwaffe knew it had met its match. On July 14, 1944 a force of 18 Yak-3s met 30 German fighters and destroyed 15 Luftwaffe aircraft for the loss of only one of their own. As the more powerful 1700hp VK-107 engine became available, Yakovlev installed a small number into existing airframes and the Yak-3 achieved ultimate capability with a top speed of 720kph/447mph.

TOP, ABOVE RIGHT AND ABOVE: **The Yak-3 was an excellent fighter aircraft that could give a very good account of itself against any enemy aircraft of the time. Since the end of the Cold War, more Yak-3s have been rebuilt to fly for customers in the West.**

Yakovlev Yak-3

First flight: Late 1943
Power: Klimov 1300hp VK-105PF-2 piston engine
Armament: One 20mm/0.78in cannon firing through the propeller hub, plus two synchronized 12.7mm/0.5in machine-guns
Size: Wingspan – 9.2m/30ft 2.25in
Length – 8.49m/27ft 10.25in
Height – 2.42m/7ft 11.25in
Wing area – 14.83m^2/159.63sq ft
Weights: Empty – 2105kg/4641lb
Maximum take-off – 2660kg/5864lb
Performance: Maximum speed – 655kph/407mph
Ceiling – 10,700m/35,105ft
Range – 900km/559 miles
Climb – 1300m/4265ft per minute

ABOVE: **Yak-7Bs of the Red Air Force. The B model was built in great numbers, with a total of around 5000 reaching front-line units.** RIGHT: **A Yak-3 of an unknown Soviet fighter regiment.** BELOW RIGHT: **Before it took delivery of Yak-9s, the Free French Normandie-Niemen Group were equipped with Yak-3s.**

The Yak-7 was designed as a dual control fighter trainer and displayed such excellent flying qualities (better than the Yak-1 fighter) that a single-seat fighter version was ordered into production and over 5000 were built in all.

The Yak-9 was designed in parallel with the Yak-3 and was a development of an experimental Yak-7. Production of the Yak-9 began in October 1942 and differed from the earlier Yak by having light metal alloy spars in the wings.

The type became a significant factor in the air battles over Stalingrad where it met and outclassed the Messerschmitt Bf109G. The Free French Normandie-Niemen Group that flew with the Soviet Air Force and Free Polish squadrons were both equipped with the Yak-9. By mid-1943, the aircraft was incorporating more and more aluminium to save weight and increase strength. Fitted with increasingly more powerful versions of the VK-105 engine, the various variants include the standard Yak-9M, the long-range Yak-9D. The very long-range Yak-9DD was used to escort USAAF bombers and some even flew from the Ukraine to southern Italy to aid partisans.

The final major variant of the Yak-9 was the all-metal Yak-9U, first flown in December 1943, that entered service in the latter half of 1944. At first the Yak-9U was fitted with the VK-105PF-2 engine but the VK-107A engine was introduced later giving a maximum speed of 698kph/434mph. Even the early -9Us were able to outfly any fighters the Germans cared to field. The Yak-9 remained in production well into 1946 and was the most numerous of all the wartime Yak fighters with 16,769 built. When the Korean War began in 1950, the post-war cannon-armed Yak-9P was the most advanced fighter in the North Korean Air Force inventory.

Total production of the wartime Yak fighter series was in excess of 37,000.

Yakovlev Yak-9U

First flight: Late 1943

Power: Klimov 1650hp VK-107A in-line piston engine

Armament: One 20mm/0.78in cannon firing through hub plus two 12.7mm/0.5in machine-guns and two 100kg/220lb bombs under wings

Size: Wingspan – 9.77m/32ft 0.75in
Length – 8.55m/28ft 0.5in
Height – 2.96m/9ft 8.5in
Wing area – 17.25m^2/185.68sq ft

Weights: Empty – 2716kg/5988lb
Maximum take-off – 3098kg/6830lb

Performance: Maximum speed – 698kph/434mph
Ceiling – 11,900m/39,040ft
Range – 870km/541 miles
Climb – 1500m/4920ft per minute

Acknowledgements

The author would like to give special thanks to Mike Bowyer, Peter March, Kazuko Matsuo and Hideo Kurihara for their help with picture research.

The publisher would like to thank the following individuals and picture libraries for the use of their pictures in the book (l=left, r=right, t=top, b=bottom, m=middle, um=upper middle, lm=lower middle). Every effort has been made to acknowledge the pictures properly, however we apologize if there are any unintentional omissions, which will be corrected in future editions.

Michael J.F. Bowyer: 25tl; 31b; 37t; 42t; 44b; 47b; 48t; 58b; 69bl; 75bl; 79m; 85mr.
Francis Crosby Collection: 44t; 56b; 63b; 68t; 92b; 123b.
Imperial War Museum Photograph Archive: 10t (Q 67436); 10b (Q 67062); 11t (Q 67832); 12t (Q 69593); 12r (Q 42283); 13m (Q 114172); 13b (Q 64214); 14tr (Q 28180); 15tr (Q 68415); 15b (TR 516); 17tl (CH 3513); 17tr (EA 34177A); 18r (Q 63125); 19t (FRA 102960); 19m (TR 22); 19b (FRA 102079); 20t (HU 2742); 21l (GER 530); 22 (TR 139); 23tl (HU 1215); 23tr (HU 50153); 23b (CH 1299); 24b (CL 2332); 25tr (CH 16117); 25br (CH 16607); 27tl (TR 285); 27tr (NYF 18669); 27m (NYF 74296); 27b (A 9423); 30tr (Q 61061); 34t (CH 886); 34b (CH 1101); 35t (COL 187); 35bl (CH 5105); 35br (TR 868); 36b (MH 165); 39t (Q79081); 39m (Q 68344); 39b (Q 11993); 40t (Q 66585); 42b (MH 5698); 43b (TR 978); 45tl (Q 11897); 46b (ATP 12184F); 47t (HU 1642); 49t (HU 2840); 51t (MA 6711); 51lm (HU 2395); 51b (MH 4190); 52b (Q 33847); 54b (Q 63153); 61tl (TR 284); 61tr (A 11644); 61b (A 24528); 63t (NYF 28563); 65m; 67tr (CH 5093); 67m (C 1291); 67b (CH 17331); 70m (MH 4881); 76t (EA 15161); 77t (OEM 5182); 79tr (CH 15662); 79b (HU 2742); 80b (HU 5181); 81m (HU 2741); 81b (MH 4908); 82 (CT 842); 89tl (HU 63024); 89tr (HU 63022); 89bl (CF 899); 89br (HU 63021); 92t (C 1378); 93tr (Q 55974); 101m (CH 7059); 101b (NYP 21768A); 109m (HU 31375); 109br (EA 25060); 111um (Q 60550); 111b (Q 60608); 112t (Q 07104); 112m (Q 67249); 112b (Q 69650); 115tl (Q 67556); 115tr (Q 27508); 115bl (Q 57660); 115br (HU 68205); 117t (HU 39323); 118m (Q 67061); 120t (COL 188); 121tl (CH 24); 121m (TR 23); 121b (PMA 20625); 123um (A 25442); 123lm (A20026); 125m (RR 2219).
Key Publishing Ltd: 32b; 33b.
Cliff Knox: 11um; 14b; 16; 24t; 36t; 38b; 48b; 53b; 62bl; 66t; 66b; 67tl; 76b; 77m; 78t; 93b; 98t; 114t; 118b; 122t; 123t; 124b.
Kokujoho Magazine: 96um; 96lm.
Hideo Kurihara: 88b; 95t.
Daniel J. March: 26t; 45tr.
Peter R. March: 1; 2–3; 4; 7; 11lm; 11b; 12l; 13t; 14tl; 18l; 20b; 21tr; 21br; 25bl; 26b; 28–9; 30tl; 32t; 33t; 37b; 38t; 40b; 41b; 43t; 46t; 49m; 51um; 52t; 53t; 54t; 55b; 56t; 57t; 57m; 57b; 58t; 59t; 60t; 60b; 62t; 63m; 64t; 64bl; 65t; 65b; 68b; 69br; 70b; 71t; 72t; 72b; 73t; 73m; 74m; 77b; 78b; 79tl; 80t; 81t; 83t; 84t; 84b; 85ml; 85b; 86b; 87; 88t; 91t; 91b; 93tl; 94b; 95b; 96t; 97b; 98m; 98b; 99t; 99b; 100t; 100b; 103t; 104t; 107t; 107m; 108t; 108b; 109t; 109bl; 110t; 110b; 111t; 113t; 113b; 114b; 116b; 117b; 118t; 119t; 119m; 119b; 120b; 121tr; 122b; 124t; 124m; 127.
Maru Magazine: 74t; 74b; 94t; 97tr.
Northrop Grumman: 15tl; 59b; 62br; 64br.
Bruce Robertson: 30b; 41t; 45b; 49b; 73b; 75t; 83b; 86t; 90t; 90b; 96b; 97tl; 104b; 106t; 106b; 107b; 116t; 125t; 125b.
Geoff Sheward: 101t; 105t; 105b.
Brian Strickland Collection: 31t; 50; 55t; 69t; 70t; 71b; 75br; 85t; 102; 103b; 111lm.

Index

Notes

Notes

Notes